Marketing With Newsletters

How to Boost Sales, Add Members,
Raise Donations & Further Your Cause
With a Promotional Newsletter

Elaine Floyd

COMMUNICATIONS

Marketing With Newsletters: How to Boost Sales, Win Members, Raise Donations & Further Your Cause With a Promotional Newsletter.

Library of Congress Cataloging-in-Publication Data

Floyd, Elaine, 1961-
    Marketing with newsletters: how to boost sales, add members, raise donations and
    further your cause with a promotional newsletter / Elaine Floyd.--
       p. cm.
    Includes bibliographical references and index.
    ISBN: 0-9630222-0-2
    1. Newsletters--Publishing.   2. Marketing.   I. Title.
Z286.N46   070.175
            QB191-1295
            MARC

First Edition, Second Printing

Printed and bound in the United States of America.

EF Communications   SAN 297-4541
6614 Pernod Ave.
St. Louis, MO 63139-2149
(800) 264-6305; (314) 647-6788

Dedication

Marketing With Newsletters is dedicated to the many businesspeople who helped develop these ideas and let me try them in their newsletters. It's also dedicated to the newsletter editors, trainers and writers I spoke with while working on this project. Through your willingness to share ideas and your encouragement (telling me you'd buy a copy), you made this book possible.

Acknowledgements

To all of the people who helped with this book, I could use the copy/paste function to duplicate "thank you" thousands of times. To conserve paper, I'll just say, "Thanks."

Mike Wells and Shaun Frongillo provided corrections, comments and encouragement for the first version of the manuscript.

Mark Beach and Kathleen Ryan of Coast to Coast Books, along with Elizabeth Collins and KiKi Canniff, provided the suggestions and editing that converted the original manuscript into the book that's in your hands.

Editing, insight on newsletter design and comments on the use of promotional newsletters for corporate communicators were given by Polly Pattison of Pattison Workshops.

Final manuscript editing was completed by Donn Silvis, ABC, Associate Professor of Communications; California State University, Dominguez Hills.

The cartoons ("Rufus & the Ducks") were drawn by Alexandre Todorov.

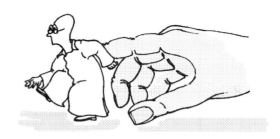

Hey,
You Skimmers
Out There

This will just take a second…

Since much of this book is dedicated to communication with skimmers of newsletters, it would be rude to ignore you book skimmers.

There's just one thing you need to know.

Throughout the book, communicating with readers is compared to leading prospects and customers up a mountain. The basic idea is to lead readers through four stages, collectively called RISE:

> ➤ **RECOGNITION**: telling people who you are, where to find you, and what you provide.

> ➤ **IMAGE**: showing that you can provide what your prospects want, that you run a good business and that you are an expert at what you do.

> ➤ **SPECIFICS**: giving specific features and reasons why your prospects should choose your product, service or cause over those of your competitors.

> ➤ **ENACTMENT**: telling readers what action to take—return the reply card, call your toll free number, or send in an order or donation.

Okay, now you know what RISE and mountain climbing have to do with promotional newsletters.

Feel free to skim, skip and flip through the chapters at your leisure.

Note to Non-Marketing Editors

For editors of church newsletters and internal corporate publications (employee newsletters, and so forth), this book contains valuable information you can use to attract the attention of your readers. I hope you'll take no offense to my "sales and marketing" use of newsletters and will look for ideas you can use to better serve your community of readers.

Table of Contents

3

4

5

6

Scouting Out Readers' Interests 71

7

Mailing Lists: Choosing the Best Mountain Climbers 93

8

9

10

11

12

13

Put Your Newsletter Dollars to Work

All kinds of organizations market themselves with newsletters. Small businesses and large corporations use them. Consultants, doctors, lawyers, accountants, real estate and insurance agents, associations, schools, hospitals, churches, charities, and more, all promote their products, services and ideas through newsletters.

You can, too. All it takes is some planning and fine-tuned marketing skills.

Promotional newsletters are powerful. They are the ideal marketing tool to spread information promoting today's products and services. They also win the votes, donations and volunteer time of community members.

As you can see, the term "promotional" includes any reader reaction that benefits your organization. It often includes, but isn't limited to, direct sales dollars. Take a glance at some successful newsletter publishers.

➤ A non-profit organization needed volunteers to serve holiday dinners to the homeless. By publishing a special Christmas edition of the newsletter, the group recruited 200 volunteers and generated $10,000 in donations.

➤ A business association decided to upgrade its newsletter and increase the distribution. By boosting its publication budget by $300 per month, its meeting attendance rose from 250 to 550 people in the first year. Excluding the extra $3,600 spent upgrading the newsletter, new membership dues added over $50,000 to the coffers.

➤ A computer parts manufacturer invested $3,000 on a 10,000 circulation newsletter produced to introduce its new product line. The sales leads generated by the newsletter created $300,000 in sales within 30 days.

This book shows you how to maximize your newsletter's promotional value. It contains practical information for editors with all levels of experience.

➤ For editors of existing newsletters, it provides new ideas to use immediately.

➤ For editors of new publications, it offers several methods to maximize marketing results from the start.

➤ For first-time editors, it explains the basics, then cuts through the "learning curve" to make your first newsletter a promotional success.

You Need This Book!

You, or your organization, are probably spending or getting ready to spend a few hundred to several thousand dollars on each issue of your newsletter. What do your publishing dollars buy? Lots, with the planning and marketing techniques shown in the coming pages.

Whether you are a professional communicator looking for marketing pointers or an experienced marketer needing help with the tasks involved in writing and editing a newsletter, this manual explains both sales techniques and basic newsletter editing so you can get the most out of your money and time.

It helps you:

➤ discover sales and marketing methods you can immediately put to work in your newsletter

➤ learn skills that make newsletter editing and production run smoothly

➤ find out how to put it all together into targeted news that promotes your products, services and ideas

Here's What You Get

This book contains 13 chapters. The first two provide basic information on both marketing and newsletters. These fundamentals guide you through each decision you will need to make throughout the book.

The next chapter presents the four marketing levels of promotional newsletters. There, you'll find many examples demonstrating how newsletters can benefit your organization.

Chapters 4 through 8 tell how to apply everything you've learned to your own newsletter. You'll learn how to set goals for your newsletter and match them to your customers' and prospects' interests. You'll also learn how to choose new prospects for your mailing list and how to tap the marketing power of computers. Then, you'll use this knowledge to create an appealing and effective newsletter.

Finally, you'll learn design, writing and layout techniques that cause readers to respond. You'll learn methods for publishing newsletters and how to use your newsletter information to promote your organization in other ways.

I hope the information you need is easy to find, fun to learn, and immediately applicable to the promotion of your organization. Your comments are encouraged and appreciated.

Elaine Floyd
New Orleans, July 1991

1
Fundamentals for Promotional Newsletters

Every year many newsletters find their way into your mailbox. They are sent by your employer, church, professional association, doctor or local politician. Some of them you read; others you just throw away.

You read the ones that pique your interest. Your senator's newsletter reveals the inside scoop at the Capitol. Your doctor's publication advises you on how to stay healthy. Your church or company newsletter brings news of the people you like and a calendar of upcoming activities. These are promotional newsletters.

Promotional newsletters are interesting and inviting. This chapter gives you an overview of what a promotional newsletter is and how to set the foundation for your newsletter's success.

Newsletters Invite Action

All newsletters promote specific goals. Association and church publications strive to gain new members and retain existing ones. Public relations newsletters attempt to sway your support toward an industry, a political party, or an issue. Internal newsletters promote the goals of an organization. Charities use newsletters to increase donations or volunteer time. In general, newsletters are successful for the following tasks:

> ➤ bring in new supporters
> ➤ sell more to existing customers

> improve morale
> inform and educate
> increase involvement
> attract volunteers
> bring back lost customers
> win support
> boost donations
> unify a "community" of readers

In order to achieve these goals, however, newsletters have to be read. The newsletters people read contain useful information presented in appropriate and appealing ways. Successful promotional newsletters get people to read not only what interests them, but also what the publisher wants them to read.

Two Signs of Success

Successful promotional newsletters keep sight of two things:

> the readers' interests
> the publication's goals

Targeted content and design attract readers. Volunteers want recognition, purchasing agents want prices, salespeople want ideas that help them sell more. Publication budgets vary between organizations. Print your charity newsletter on low-cost paper so donors feel their money is frugally spent. Print your accounting newsletter on crisp, heavy paper to impress prospective clients.

When environmental awareness first began to heighten, many newsletter editors scrambled to find recycled paper for their publication. For environment-related newsletters, the notice "printed on recycled paper" was necessary to avoid an influx of reader protests.

At the same time, use design and content to meet your organization's goals. For example, while a newsletter on Washington politics contains the latest inside stories, the sponsoring politician's name and achievements are also prominently displayed. This way voters read the entire publication while knowing whom it's from. While most readers prefer looking at color pictures over black and white, newsletters are usually printed using only one or two ink colors. The money saved on printing can be spent increasing newsletter distribution.

Before going into details, let's look at an overview of how promotional newsletters are put together. Each step is vital to maintaining the promotional value of your newsletter.

Keeping a Finger on the Promotional Pulse

Creating a promotional newsletter requires two steps. First, design all the things that stay consistent from issue to issue. After that's done, each time you create a new issue, you do tasks such as collecting photographs, writing articles, and so on.

Get a feel for the steps involved. At first they may seem straightforward, but each step influences the resulting promotional power of your newsletter. Think "promotion" during each step. Subsequent chapters cover how you accomplish each one. When you first develop your newsletter, do the following things:

➢ **Set Promotional Goals for Your Newsletter.** Your promotional goals state how you want the newsletter to affect your marketing efforts. They must be measurable, realistic and timely in order to know if they were accomplished or not. For example, the goal of a small business may be to have 75% of its potential audience recognize it as an industry leader. The goals of an insurance agent can be to increase word of mouth referrals by a certain percent. Your goal can even be as straightforward as increasing donations or revenue by 25% within six months.

➢ **Identify Audience & Set Up a Mailing List.** Decide who you want as a supporter, whom you want to sell more to, or who can help you promote your organization. This is your audience. Put them on your list. Then, store your mailing list in a computerized database. This makes it easy to sort information by zip code, customer type, and any other attributes important to your business. In addition, purchase other organization's lists that contain the same type of prospects.

➢ **Research Audience Interests.** To attract the attention of your readers, find out what they want to read—their "hot buttons." You can survey your prospective readers over the telephone, in person, or through a mail questionnaire. In a matter of days, you can have enough feedback to create a newsletter that people will read.

➢ **Develop Content.** The content of your newsletter serves two purposes. It captures the attention of your prospects and it motivates them to respond to your promotional message. To be successful, however, strike a balance between newsworthy information and your promotional news.

➤ **Set a Budget.** Plan for the amount of time and money required. Study ways to save time through subcontracting. Look into ways to cut costs such as publishing a smaller newsletter. With accurate budgeting, your publication can be produced regularly without creating a financial burden on your organization.

➤ **Name Your Newsletter.** The name and subtitle of your newsletter state the benefit of reading the publication. The subtitle tells for whom the newsletter is written. For example, the name of a financial planner's newsletter can be *Retirement Riches* with the subtitle, "News for investors who want financial security after 65."

➤ **Create a Design.** The design of your newsletter is the first thing your reader sees. In essence, it's your "calling card." Match your newsletter's style and color to your organization's image. Graphic consultants are often called in to design a first issue template which the editor can implement with future issues.

As you develop each issue of the newsletter, follow these steps:

➤ **Plan Content.** Provide eye-catching content that achieves your goals in each issue. Provide at least a few pieces of timely information. This encourages prospects to read the publication immediately rather than saving it for later.

➤ **Collect Information.** Gather information by interviewing, researching other publications, and finding sources within your organization. Choose facts and features that enhance your marketing message and interest your readers.

➤ **Find Visuals.** An effective visual can communicate a concept faster than any other method. Create or find photographs, clip art, charts, etc., that visually reinforce your promotional message.

➤ **Write Articles, Headlines, Captions, etc.** In a concise writing style, present the information your prospects need. Include news summaries and blurbs. Write headlines and captions that capture readers' interest. In longer articles, use subheads and graphics that make reading fun.

➤ **Edit and Proofread.** Assure correct spelling and accurate information. This increases the quality of your newsletter and gives prospects confidence in your organization.

➤ **Typeset and Layout.** Type, typeset, or laser-print your text. Combine the text with visuals in a way that leads readers through the entire newsletter and makes them pause to read your promotional messages.

➤ **Print.** Choose a printer who can give you the quality you want. Provide the printer with high-quality photographs, camera-ready layout, and instructions.

➤ **Label, Sort and Mail.** Find the most cost effective and appropriate method of mailing. Follow all mailing regulations to assure expeditious delivery of each newsletter.

➤ **Follow Up.** Thank contributors and vendors involved with each issue. This assures cooperation for upcoming ones. Immediately follow up on the responses your newsletter generates.

It's a lot to keep up with. As you work through the remainder of the book you'll learn how to complete each of these steps.

Depending on the type of promotional newsletter you choose, you may be concerned with only part of the list. For example, if you're a real estate agent and plan on using the newsletter to initiate personal sales calls to homeowners, you won't mail the publication. You won't have to worry about setting up a mailing list. If you decide to publish one page of text straight off your word processor and photocopied onto your letterhead, you won't be concerned with typesetting or printing.

Support From Within Your Organization

The best way to assure your newsletter reflects the image and goals of your organization is by having an internal support team. While many newsletters are produced using outside vendors, the internal team keeps the publication on its promotional track. The managing editor is the leader of the team and an editorial board is the support.

Managing Editor's Responsibilities. The managing editor assures that each newsletter is published on a regular basis and oversees the preparation of the entire publication. The editor is in charge of setting deadlines, writing or finding writers for the chosen articles, editing copy, and monitoring the typesetting, layout, printing and distribution.

To manage a promotional newsletter you must have good writing skills, an understanding of your readers, efficient work habits and organizational skills.

Because you deal with news, trade issues, and trends as they relate to your targeted audience, you must know the subject well. You should also have the ability to write in a way that reflects the image of your organization. You also need the organizational skills to maintain the budget and to set up the staff structure and production schedule.

Enormous enthusiasm for the project, the capacity to control the promotional tone of the piece, and most importantly, the ability to motivate vendors, staff, volunteers and readers are all essential attributes of a managing editor.

Editorial Board's Responsibilities. The editorial board is responsible for keeping the marketing functions of the newsletter in focus. The group typically critiques each issue and provides new article ideas. The team also sets up the long-range marketing plans for the publication, including a yearly editorial schedule.

The board can consist of as few or as many people as are needed to get the job done. It all depends on the size and structure of your organization. It might include sales representatives, board members, technical experts or senior partners, marketing and public relations people, writers and other production staff.

Each member is responsible for suggesting, checking and reviewing a specific part of the newsletter. An engineering manager may be asked to check for technical accuracy and suggest articles on certain product features. The president, CEO, or board members scrutinize the newsletter for consistency with the organization's image and policies.

The composition of the editorial board will vary from organization to organization. The board for a promotional newsletter of a local United Way agency may contain the editor, the agency's director, and the representative in charge of contributions. A division of a Fortune 500 company may have a board comprised of the newsletter editor, the sales manager, the vice president of research and development, the division manager, the marketing manager and the account executive of its advertising agency. Some organizations invite a customer or avid supporter to participate.

> **The board for an internal corporate newsletter may be the editor and the editor's supervisor.**

While your board can be made up of several representatives, it's important to keep it lean. Educate all board members on the promotional aims and policies of the newsletter. Give everyone a style sheet. For the benefit of your sanity, thoroughly define the responsibilities of each person.

During newsletter production, the publication should receive top priority from each member. Everyone must strive to approve each issue promptly. Forty-eight hours is the maximum time for the entire approval process for most newsletters.

With modern technology, like facsimile machines and modems, it's not even necessary for the board to physically meet around the same conference table. For organizations spread across the country or the world, article suggestions can be given over the phone, wording and layout approved by sending board members copies, and so on. It is helpful, though, to have everyone together at least once a year to discuss the next year's editorial plan. A good time for this may be at your yearly conference or trade show.

With the foundation for your promotional newsletter firmly in place, let's move on to more specific information on how your newsletter can be used to promote your organization.

2
Marketing Techniques for Editors

Sales and marketing are the keys to the survival and growth of any organization. It's an ongoing effort to keep existing clients coming back and to turn prospects into customers. Successful marketing also turns current customers into better customers.

This chapter discusses sales and marketing in detail. It helps you target your best prospects and tells how to send them your promotional messages.

Who Are Your Prospects?

Anyone who doesn't use your services is a prospect. Customers not using *all* of your services are better prospects.

This is the universal rule of "80/20" that works for any organization. The rule is that 80 percent of your sales, volunteer time, billings or donations come from 20 percent of your customers, members, patients or donors. You've noticed this firsthand if you've ever been actively involved with any group or association. Out of a group of 100 people, the same 20 people are the ones who hold offices, volunteer for clean-up duty, attend meetings and so on.

It's imperative to keep customers in mind as prime prospects for additional products and services. For instance, the couple delivering their firstborn at your hospital are now prospects for your other family services. You can provide them infor-

By concentrating on current customers for new business, you get more for your marketing dollars. Marketing to existing customers is five times less expensive than winning new ones. Your response rate is higher because you know who your customers are and your customers know you.

mation on exercise programs, infant nutrition classes, emergency and outpatient services, family counseling and any number of other family-oriented services. Because the couple is familiar with the quality and atmosphere of your hospital, and has already chosen your hospital once, they will feel comfortable coming back. They are much better prospects than people who have never used your facility.

While it's important to keep your existing clients, you need to replenish your customer base with new faces. Even the best-run organizations suffer some attrition. Members and volunteers move out of town, businesses close down, your best client moves its advertising in-house, your competitors take some of your customers. It happens.

Marketing to customers and prospects through a newsletter follows basic principles of communications.

When choosing your newsletter's content, first look at the hard news you have for supporters and prospects—new services, special events and so on. Then search for information that keeps readers involved and interested in your subject— "how to's," other people's products, worksheets, calendars, etc. These increase your newsletter's value and keep prospects reading time after time.

Communication is Vital to Marketing

In recent years, most marketplaces have become increasingly competitive. Small merchants have lost business to major chains. Promoting through a direct sales force is often cost prohibitive and many companies sell by telephone.

The result is that most of us have unpleasant images of salespeople. You think of the pushy car dealer who uses high pressure techniques to sell you the lemon that's always in the shop; the shoe salesperson who barks at you from across the store; the telephone solicitor who interrupts your family dinner.

Effective promotions don't have to be done that way. Instead, sales can be made through effective communication. Good salespeople are experts on their products and services. They know the technology, as well as the capabilities and structure of their organization. They are also experts on the needs and wants of their customers. They know how to present information in a concise, useful manner. They also know the importance of assuring customers they won't be abandoned after the purchase.

You can market your products, services, causes and ideas the same way through a newsletter. The key is in the content you choose.

The Content Makes the Sale

One of the first questions asked when setting up a promotional newsletter is, "what am I going to write about?" The next is, "do I have enough to say on an ongoing basis?"

For instance, the owner of a violin shop is interested in starting a newsletter but isn't sure what to include. The store receives new products frequently but not often enough to devote an entire newsletter to them. Should the proprietor abandon the project? Not just yet.

The shopkeeper should be providing promotional information that goes beyond just new product releases. The information can include anything which keeps prospects interested in music—new classical music on compact disc, announcements of symphony performances, a list of area music teachers, maintenance tips for violins, muscle strengthening exercises, the importance of posture, etc.

Similar examples exist for other industries and markets.

A New Mexico senator working in Washington D.C. stays in touch with the folks back home through a newsletter. The *Washington Report* includes summaries of political actions taking place in the Capitol. It also brings the senator's activities closer to home by showing a local park developed with federal funds. To help the senator better represent the people, readers are asked to complete and return questionnaires listing their views on current political issues.

An association of stamp collectors publishes a newsletter to increase attendance of current members at its meetings. It also includes articles on the joys of stamp collecting in hopes of interesting new members. To extend membership to children, the group buys a mailing list and sends three different issues to area school teachers. The newsletters for teachers include a special educational insert with a lesson plan for teaching kids about stamps. The newsletter's design gives readers a feeling for stamps.

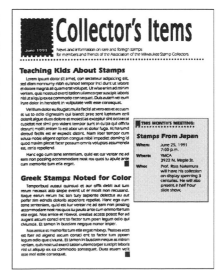

A dentist sends a newsletter to the residents in the surrounding area to promote his painless techniques for wisdom tooth extraction. The newsletter includes an educational article from the hygienist on why it's important to have teeth cleaned every six months. A discount coupon for $5 off tooth cleaning is placed next to the article.

Depending on market conditions, some of these newsletters will be able to sell services, attract members, and win community support without additional marketing. Others need to be combined with such marketing efforts as face-to-face visits, direct mail, conventions and telemarketing.

The Four Marketing Levels of Promotional Newsletters

Publishing a newsletter taps into your most vital marketing resources—time and money. Before deciding to commit either one, make sure a newsletter will benefit your promotional efforts and facilitate two-way communication.

One of the factors affecting the benefits gained from publishing is the degree of "reader interaction" you achieve. Like a guide leading hikers up a mountain, involve your readers and encourage them to keep reading (or climbing). This way you lead your prospects from the valley and up to the top of the mountain where they become customers. But gravity, like laziness, encourages readers to stop climbing. Your job is to be an interesting tour guide and give readers the information they need to keep the climb interesting and challenging, yet painless.

In other words, you want to take readers from Prospect Valley to Customer Mountain. In your newsletter, you move your prospects up the mountain by conveying information using the best techniques available.

Reader interaction techniques can be broken down to coincide with four levels of promotion. Combine these levels and your readers RISE from prospects to ardent supporters. Here are the four steps to RISE:

➤ **RECOGNITION**. Your prospects need basic awareness of your organization before they can do business with you. Tell them who you are, where to find you, and, in general, what products or services you provide.

➤ **IMAGE**. You must project a professional image. In the initial stages of a purchasing decision, your prospects carefully evaluate your organization. Why should they place an order, make an appointment, or give a donation to you instead of someone else? Prove that you run a credible business. Show that you're an expert.

➤ **SPECIFICS**. At this level, your prospects and customers want more information on why they should support you. Give specific features and reasons why they should choose you over your competitors. Make a marketing presentation.

➤ **ENACTMENT**. Without a call to action, there can be no sale. Once your prospects are ready to act, tell them what to do. Cast your vote this Tuesday. Call this toll free number now. Return this reply card. Write your legislator today. Send $25 to help feed a family of four.

Depending on the goals and abilities of your organization and the needs of your prospects and customers, a newsletter can effectively lead your readers through each level of RISE. The following four chapters detail each of the four promotional levels.

3

Promote With Every Element

The four levels of RISE—recognition, image, specifics and enactment—show how promotional newsletters market your organization. This chapter takes you through an overview of each promotional level and lists the newsletter elements used at each one. Determine which type of promotional help your organization needs most. Writing, design and layout of each element are discussed later in the book.

Recognition: Making initial contact

You must lure your recipients out of their daily routine and on to your "trail" up the mountain. Coax them into reading your newsletter.

The first obstacle you must overcome is building name recognition with your prospects. Your newsletter needs to lock your organization's name, products and services into your prospects' minds. You want them to know you at first glance.

If you're unsure of how to accomplish this, keep reading and study the strategies of companies who seem to have their name *everywhere*.

Look at Coca-Cola. Granted, it has a huge advertisement budget for TV, radio and print advertisements. But look closer at its other marketing. Coca-Cola machines are at every gas station and snack area. Coca-Cola refrigerators are in mini-markets. It even has people paying for clothing featuring its logo.

Another example is Rock City. If you've traveled by car within 500 miles of Chattanooga, TN, you'll recognize the slogan "see Rock City." I'm not sure what

Rock City is, beyond a tourist attraction, but drivers are bombarded with bumper stickers on cars, billboards and signs painted on barns. "See Rock City" is painted everywhere motorists look. Though not everyone drives up the Chattanooga ridges to "see" Rock City, the attraction has achieved the first stage in effective marketing: a large percentage of its prospects know its name and location. That's the first step in getting them there.

This stage of marketing gives prospects all of the basic information they need to know to do business with you. They want to know who you are, where and when to find you, and what products or services you offer.

How to Get Recognized

When your newsletter arrives in the mail, the recipient glances to see whom it's from. Here, your newsletter has just unobtrusively reminded your current and future customers, members, or patients of your existence. It can help them recall an upcoming event or a brochure you previously sent. Your name enters your prospects' minds as soon as they glance at the return address.

At this level, your newsletter works as a recognition tool. It's simply a regularly-produced direct mail piece keeping your name in front of your prospects. Though the concept is discouraging to hard-working writers, a large part of your newsletter's promotional value is not the quality of the articles but the cumulative effect of planting your organization's name into your prospect's brain, time and time again.

Almost all recipients will stay on your trail through the beginning of the recognition level. Make their first few steps count. Use the mailing panel and nameplate of your newsletter to give readers more than just your organization's name and address.

Place any information that might spur interest in your products, services or causes in the mailing panel. Use any of these:

> ➤ your organization's logo
> ➤ your slogan
> ➤ a location map (if important to prospects)
> ➤ a list of your products and services
> ➤ a highlight of the volunteer of the month
> ➤ an advertisement for a monthly special
> ➤ teasers to encourage the recipients to open the newsletter *now*

Once your prospects have looked at the mailing panel, many turn to the front page. They have just jumped several steps up the trail and are standing in front of the "you are here" sign—the nameplate. The nameplate signals the starting place for the newsletter content. It also gives words of encouragement telling why the reader should continue on the journey.

Through the nameplate you catch readers' interest with:

> ➤ a newsletter name explaining the benefits of further reading
> ➤ a subtitle that says your newsletter is written just for them
> ➤ a nameplate design telling more about what you do

The name of your newsletter should state why prospects should read further. For example, a charity's newsletter for prospective volunteers and donors, *Making a Difference*, tells readers the result of their support. The title of a manufacturer's newsletter, *Retail Success*, explains why the retailers should read the publication. Not all newsletter names can include benefits. If you can't include a benefit in your title, put the newsletter's subject in the title. Identify the benefit and targeted reader in the subtitle.

A subtitle is a promotional opportunity you should never pass up. The subtitle allows you to keep the title short, which can then be set in large (over 72 point) type. If the newsletter's name includes a benefit, the subtitle includes the subject and readers. If the name tells the subject, the subtitle explains the benefit and reader.

The subtitle of *Making a Difference* is "How your time and donations are improving the lives of the homeless." For *Retail Success*, it's "The latest product news and sales ideas for retailers of home furnishings." If the title of your newsletter is the subject, then the subtitle contains the benefit and the reader. For example, *Underground Storage Tank Update* has the subtitle "The only news source that helps fuel distributors comply with EPA regulations."

A software publisher reproduces its company logo in the mailing panel to increase recognition. It also adds a graphic which sets the mood for the rest of its light-spirited newsletter. Below the graphic in a small box, a note tells readers that the company's word processing program was used to produce the newsletter. Now, the rest of the newsletter works as a testimonial for the product.

The title and the subtitle come together in the design of the nameplate. The nameplate sets the tone of your publication through the typestyle, its size and position, and any other graphic elements used. For example, a foundation for housing preservation designed a nameplate featuring a sketch of houses with architectures unique to the city. The foundation's mission of preserving this community asset is communicated graphically.

Many of your prospects join your marketing path somewhere en route. They already recognize your name and are further along the trail than other readers. Avoid having them return to "Start." Design your nameplate to look like your other promotions. Use your organization's logo or a familiar design in the nameplate.

Familiar slogans can also be worked into the newsletter nameplate. One chapter of the YMCA uses its slogan as the name of its newsletter, *Still Changing Lives*. State Farm's newsletter for customers and prospects is *The Good Neighbor*. Taking some familiar examples, the newsletter for the United Way could be called *Helping Hands* and show the outstretched palms seen at the end of most of its TV commercials.

Once readers grow familiar with your publication's "look," work on ways to make each issue arouse curiosity. This is the transition point between the recognition and image levels.

Look at the nameplate of a mailing list broker's newsletter. The title, *Direct Success*, tells the reader what benefit the newsletter offers. The subtitle tells both a benefit and the subject, "Quarterly tips & techniques for profitable direct mail marketing."

Leading Readers to the Image Level

Some readers may return to your mountain time after time with only the intention of walking the first mile. For some newsletters, such as ones listing regularly scheduled events, readers may look only for the meeting notice or calendar. Knowing that most readers are looking for this information, use teasers to lead them inside for further reading.

Convince recipients that the newsletter includes timely information they must read now. Because most people look at the front page, use teasers, such as an "inside this issue" box. Discourage readers from putting the newsletter aside with magazines and other materials they don't have time to read while opening their mail. Once your newsletter hits this stack, your climber is off the path and back in the Winnebago.

Your nameplate and mailing panel can build the recognition readers need to rise to the next level. If you can accomplish this, your chances of keeping readers on the path to image increases. You also want to convey an immediacy to the climb. Including timely information such as dates and expirations encourages readers to start the climb right away.

> The goal of a local association's newsletter is to draw its members to monthly meetings and events. The newsletter is mailed flat and uses the entire front cover to list facts about upcoming meetings. On the same page, a box lists other items in the newsletter and includes a pointing finger, suggesting that readers turn the page. ☞

Image: Dressing for success

Once you achieve name and product recognition, your prospects open up your newsletter to investigate further. They glance at the front and back pages to see if they want to read it. You have about 15 seconds to grab their attention.

The image stage is important for all organizations. Readers often move from image directly to enactment and give you the response you want. It happens simply because you've established your name in their minds as a reputable organization. An architectural firm found this out when one of its prospects called to request a bid. When the firm asked why the prospect had called, they replied that the firm's name always came up as one of the top design companies. This was directly attributable to the firm's newsletter.

When recipients glance through your publication, reading headlines, examining photos, and scanning for something eye-catching, they absorb your image. If you've used effective promotional tactics, the reader learns the type of service you offer. If the contents are worthwhile, you have a good chance of convincing your reader to continue on the climb, maybe even to call you.

The best way to communicate quickly with your readers is either with a single visual or with very few words. These include:

➤ intriguing or emotional photographs
➤ illustrations or charts that draw readers into the article
➤ promotional and descriptive captions
➤ cartoons illustrating your promotional message
➤ concise, informative calendars
➤ headlines that tell readers the benefit of reading the article
➤ subheads that list your main ideas at a glance
➤ pull quotes telling your most important promotional message

The first items readers look at in the body of your newsletter are the photographs, illustrations and other graphics. These graphic tools make a page inviting and are much less intimidating than a page of text. They beckon readers along the image path by telling stories at a glance. Interesting photos and illustrations catch and hold readers' attention long enough for them to read the caption. In the caption, identify any people in a photograph and relay your promotional point. Readers always look at the caption. Don't miss this opportunity.

Photographs should create intrigue or emotion. An animal shelter used this photograph to encourage people to adopt a pet. The promotional caption read, "Am I cute or what? There's lots more of us who need good homes so call soon." The pet was adopted by a reader of the newsletter.

Though used less than photographs, cartoons are one of the best attention-getting devices for your promotional newsletter. The cartoon format signals "fun" to readers. While only a fraction of recipients read a long article, everyone pauses to read a cartoon. Include a promotional point in a cartoon and you'll market to readers without them ever knowing it.

Calendars give readers an immediate synopsis of an organization's news. Readers can quickly skim through and make note to attend their favorite event. Design your calendar to be easily removed and posted in a prominent place.

Headlines are also used to give readers condensed information. Headlines tell readers why they should take the time to read the article. They're also used to explain your area of expertise to skimmers. For example, the newsletter of one manufacturer used a title to tell skimmers that its products were involved in the raising of the Titanic. The headline read, "Titanic Explorers' Problem Solved by Black Box."

Along with communicating through headlines, subheads also tell your message. From a graphic standpoint, subheads are included every three or four paragraphs to break up chunks of text and make a long article look easier to read. List the main points you want readers to remember from the whole article. Use this list as the basis for your subheads. This way, you reach the skimmers as well as the thorough readers.

Another method of drawing readers into reading a long article is by using pull quotes or blurbs. Use either your top promotional point or the most intriguing line of the article and use it as a pull quote.

A good illustration draws readers' attention to an article. Once readers have discovered the article's topic, they read it if it's of interest.

Build Your Image in Your Newsletter

The elements used at the image level enhance your reputation in many ways. Your newsletter's design, color and paper quality all work to reinforce your image. The content of your newsletter is also an image-building tool.

Your newsletter shows your commitment to your market and industry. This image blossoms if your organization is the only one in your market producing a newsletter. By publishing a newsletter, you reinforce the added value of doing business with your organization—when readers buy or become members, they get aftermarket support.

Another way to demonstrate market commitment is to use your publication to unify a group of people not otherwise recognized as a group. Many non-profit organizations do this to rally the community behind social causes such as fighting illiteracy or racism.

Appearing to be a leader can be especially valuable if your organization is unknown. Because most new companies are small and some people equate size with stability and reliability, newsletters can help overcome initial hurdles by showing your products and achievements in a professional way.

Prepare Skimmers to Become Readers

Invite prospects to read your newsletter. Image-building newsletters make readers want more information. The graphics and headline techniques described earlier provide readers with "points of entry." Points of entry are places for readers to start gathering more specifics. If someone isn't interested in the first article, they need to be shown something else…quickly. Remember, you only have about 15 seconds. Readers must be able to jump from point to point in your newsletter. They want to read only what interests them. If you don't allow the readers points to jump in without reading the entire publication, you'll lose them. If you do, you may guide them to discover the specifics of your products, services and ideas—the next step in RISE.

Present readers with short articles, photographs, and large headlines. Include three or four articles per page. This way, readers can find their favorite products or subjects. If one headline doesn't attract their attention, readers can skip to other photographs, captions and headlines.

Win Supporters With Specifics

Once you have successfully used the image elements to make a skimmer pause, you've elevated your reader to the specifics stage. At this level, carefully choose your information to promote your organization. Repeating the marketing basics of Chapter 2, all promotions can be done through information alone.

Within the specifics stage:

➤ introduce new products and services
➤ tell your success stories
➤ recognize top members, donors, employees or customers
➤ report on trends and statistics
➤ give "how to" information
➤ provide technical advice
➤ share inside information

Select and write all of these articles to reinforce your promotional message to clients and prospects.

New product articles fulfill the "news" requirements of a newsletter while also marketing. When you develop a new product or service or embark on a new cause, write up the details of your project in the newsletter. Let prospects know when a new product or service is available. If you're starting a new fund drive, tell prospects exactly how they can participate. List volunteer jobs available. Give starting dates and deadlines for participation. These articles reinforce other promotional efforts you're simultaneously conducting. Your prospect may receive your post card or hear your radio announcements on the same day as reading the newsletter. The more times you tell your prospect the same message, the better chance you have of winning support or business.

After your new product, service or program is in use, write about its success. Success stories are an important part of promoting your organization. They take the risk out of giving you a call by telling prospects that you've already successfully helped other people.

For manufacturers of industrial products, a success story could explain how one customer saved money by installing your new system. A non-profit organization could explain how funds are used to give job training to people who are disabled. The article could spotlight how one of its graduates is successfully employed by a local business.

United Parcel Service once used a success story to remind customers of the company's responsiveness and of the fact it has its own fleet or airplanes. The story, "UPS Helps Customers Bring Aid to Armenia," told how a UPS plane was the first to land with relief supplies for Armenian earthquake victims.

Giving people recognition is an effective way to keep them loyal to your organization. This can be seen by the number of customer appreciation events sponsored by companies. Recognizing members and donors is especially important for non-profit organizations. People donating their time and money usually do so because they support your cause. But, chances are, they support other causes as well. Keep their attention by giving them yours. Write articles on your best supporters or customers.

Research findings are another way to attract attention. As long as the survey covers a subject that's interesting to your readers, everyone will read the results. You may have several sources within your organization for generating such reports. Design owner registration cards or membership forms with specific data you can compile for your report. The research doesn't even have to be your own. Look for it in industry publications and reports.

One marketing company used research findings to remind prospects about the need for gifts to customers. The cover article told readers about Christmas being the top time for business gift giving. The inside pages presented products like pens and coffee mugs that organizations could print their name on and give to prospects.

Other organizations promote their products by providing expertise in the form of "how to" information. Choose a subject which creates a need for your products or services. For example, a household accessory maker could show readers how to organize their home in eight easy steps by using their products.

Show your expertise by providing readers with inside information. People value opinions and forecasts. Any organization with a specialty is in the position to give readers an "inside" scoop. By talking with people within your industry every day, you gain insight that others, possibly even magazine reporters covering your "beat," don't have. If you sense a trend happening, share it with your readers. It will add value to your newsletter and keep prospects reading.

Specifics Enhance Other Promotions

Some of the benefits of newsletter publishing result from using your newsletter as a communications tool with other organizations.

Newsletters can be used as networking tools with other organizations in industries related to yours. With a trend toward specialization, it has become popular for non-competing groups in the same industry to build alliances to reduce R&D expenses or sales and marketing costs.

By providing information for your customers on products and services of non-competing organizations, you build goodwill with these suppliers as well as

> **According to advertising expert David Ogilvy, editorial material is three times more persuasive than advertising. While Americans have developed negative attitudes toward most advertising, they've developed positive attitudes toward informative advertising.**

your prospects by making your newsletter even more useful. For example, an advertising agency newsletter can include information on other marketing tools such as premiums or trade show booth designs. If the agency doesn't provide these services itself, it loses no business and makes the newsletter more informative to readers. In exchange, you can barter services or negotiate reciprocal editorial coverage in the non-competing organization's newsletter.

Your publication can also be used for public relations. It should provide local and industry media editors with a regular source of information about your organization and the market it serves. In addition, if a publication writes a story about your organization, you can reprint it (after receiving permission) in your newsletter.

Raise Readers from Specifics to Enactment

Once you've given readers the information they need to do business with you, you need them to respond to your message. Do this within the text of your newsletter, or refer readers to a reply card or enclosed order form. Some add a line with ordering information at the end of an article. Since this assumes everyone will read the entire newsletter (most won't), it's best to make reply options more noticeable. Separate response information by using italics or bold print. Or, highlight response information in a second color apart from the text. In these areas, tell readers what you want them to do—how to stay on the mailing list, get more information, order, contribute, join or vote.

This may be all you need to get your readers to respond. Most likely, though, more drastic action is needed. After all, the steepest part of your mountain is the last push you need to give your prospects to boost them to the summit.

Enactment: Generating the desired response

Once your newsletter has a prospect's attention, offer them specific ways to respond to your offer. Tell readers what action you want them to take and how to take it. This is done by providing:

➤ a self-mailing reply card

➤ a reply coupon the respondent clips and returns

➤ a masthead or announcement telling whom to write to for more information, how to send a letter to the editor, or how to send questions for a question and answer column

➤ a contest in which readers can send in photographs or suggestions on how to use your products

➤ a readership survey that generates content suggestions

➤ a telephone number to call

➤ hours of operation when prospects can stop by

➤ an advertisement telling how to buy a specific product or service

➤ a product list along with an order form readers can use to order immediately

You'll receive several types of response to your newsletter. Some people just want more information. For those who feel more comfortable writing than calling, reply cards, coupons, and information in the masthead make it easy to correspond with you. For those who'd rather call, your phone number or store

One company was so successful with its newsletter, it had to cancel it. No kidding. The company was growing too quickly and the newsletter was generating too many orders. The firm used a unique combination of a newsletter with a catalog inside. The first few pages of the newsletter looked like a standard newsletter. But inside, printed on different colored paper, was a four-page catalog.

All recipients of the newsletter were qualified buyers who had either responded by phone to advertisements or had sent back response cards from magazines. On receipt of the first issue, 21% of recipients ordered. The company repeated the same mailing to the same list. Even the fifth mailing received a respectable 3% response.

hours are useful. Put your phone number or hours in an advertisement and have people call about a specific offer. For those ready to order now, include an order form. Encourage people to phone in their order or send it via facsimile.

Though they increase the cost of printing, inserted reply cards have the advantage of standing out from the rest of your newsletter. Some publishers print them on a different color paper. Others insert them loosely so the cards fall into the recipients' hands when the newsletter is opened. (Caution: many people find this irritating.) Reply cards are printed on heavy paper, pre-addressed and often even have postage. This makes it easy for the reader to return the card without having to find and address an envelope.

Some marketers use the reply card to restate all of the organization's products and services. By asking readers to check off the information they need, you're repeating your organization's complete list of products or services. Even if they aren't interested in all of your services, readers see them one more time. If the need ever arises, the reply card helps remind prospects that you offer something they need.

Reply coupons are similar to inserted reply cards except that they are printed within the body of the newsletter and, hence, don't increase printing costs (except for perforations, if needed). Like a coupon you clip from the newspaper, readers have to either photocopy or cut out the form to reply. Reply coupons normally have a lower response rate because of the extra work. You can enhance the response by placing them near the article you've written that requests a response. The best placement for pulling the maximum response is in the lower right-hand corner of a right-hand page.

Some publishers want readers to reply only by calling. When readers are ready, they need to find your telephone number easily. Create an information box that includes your telephone number and, if important, your office hours.

Another important box many readers look for is the masthead. Readers who want to write or call directly to the editor or publisher look here for contact information and other facts about your newsletter. Don't miss an opportunity for reader response. Include a masthead in every newsletter.

To generate response, many newsletter publishers include an advertisement set apart from the copy within a box. These advertisements encourage readers to come in for a sale, attend a fund raiser, or meet you at a trade show.

Some newsletters include the publisher's product listing along with an order form to allow prospects to order directly from the newsletter. Most people consider newsletters a marketing vehicle that only works when combined with other promotional methods. Keep in mind that a good response for a hard-hitting direct mail piece is 3%. Since your newsletter is a more subtle marketing tool, you may not receive this rate of response. But this isn't always so. Hundreds of companies have successfully used them as their primary marketing tool.

Reap Maximum Benefit Through Your Response

Most communication experts agree that you must repeat the same information at least four different times in four different ways before you can assume that most people are aware of your message. Some marketing consultants go even further. Some believe you must connect at least seven times within an 18-month period.

As a direct response tool, newsletters can add to your marketing plan. By providing another place to repeat your message, your newsletter offers prospects another opportunity to respond.

To make your newsletter successful, you must be sure to follow up on all responses. Most of your respondents are going to buy *someone's* product or support someone's cause soon. Make it yours.

Can you visualize your prospects standing on top of your mountain, freshly converted to customers with their words, "I want to join," "I'd like to place an order," "Here's my donation for," or "I want more information," echoing through the valley?

It's time to see if we can get them there. The next two chapters help you set realistic expectations for your newsletter depending upon the resources you have available.

4

Maximize Results With a Newsletter Marketing Plan

Every newsletter is published with the hope of generating a flood of responses and support. Before you can lead your prospects up the mountain, though, you must build a path. And you can't build the path without knowing which mountain you want your readers to climb.

The mountain represents your marketing goals. These goals give you the direction you need when choosing newsletter content, design, mailing lists and other elements. This chapter shows you how to set specific goals that can be achieved within the pages of your newsletter. It also shows you how to combine the promotional efforts of your newsletter with your other marketing projects.

Set Performance Goals

In general, all promotional materials seek to:

> increase awareness of the organization

> promote products, services, ideas and causes

> maintain contact with clients, members, volunteers, employees or supporters

> contact prospects

> reinforce other promotional campaigns

Your newsletter's goals may encompass the general ones listed above, but they should also include specific goals unique to your newsletter. You may be

Many editors think of their newsletter as communications, not promotional tools. One editor for a marine association newsletter says the primary goal of his newsletter is to keep in touch with members. His secondary goal is to inform them of changes and industry news.

Is this really his goal?

After encouraging him to think further, his real goal is to maintain existing membership while attracting new members. Because the publication provides helpful, hard-to-find news to its targeted readers, the newsletter was already doing this to some extent. The editor just needed to make a few changes. For prospects, he added a special invitation to join the group in each newsletter. For existing members, he created a special feature highlighting a member and telling how the organization provides career help.

trying to maintain or increase membership of your association. Maybe you're lobbying an issue to legislators or community leaders. A service business, such as an accounting firm, may want to increase revenue without hiring additional staff. You may be trying to find work which bills at a higher hourly rate.

Newsletters are often launched to promote a new division or product line. For instance, a manufacturer selling telephone switches developed a telephone system for small businesses. It launched a newsletter specifically to market to this customer base. Similarly, when a hospital wanted to promote its new sports medicine program, it developed a fitness and injury recovery newsletter which was sent to athletes, coaches and health clubs.

If your newsletter is being used to promote your *existing* products and services, use the 80/20 rule discussed on page 9. Include your existing customers, members, donors, voters or volunteers in your promotional goals. Keep their support coming while you're converting other prospects.

Many publishers think only of existing supporters and exclude prospects. Some organizations send newsletters only to their current donors and volunteers. The newsletter should also be sent to community members not already supporting the organization.

Think about your specific goals. Why are you interested in publishing a newsletter? What do you expect it to do for you?

The following list shows how to rewrite primary goals into measurable, specific goals that can be easily promoted in your newsletter.

Association:

Goal: Increase membership	
Objectives:	**Strategy:**
Maintain existing membership and increase new membership by 15% within 6 months.	News articles summarizing key events in industry to keep members informed without having to read every industry journal. Make the newsletter a valued part of the membership. Members may join or renew for the sole benefit of receiving the newsletter.
Increase membership of industry newcomers (ages 23-35) by 20% this year.	Special features for new members help them quickly "learn the ropes" and include mini-dictionaries of industry jargon, lists of publications serving the industry, and calendars of events such as trade shows and conferences.
Increase meeting attendance to generate revenues.	Notices and write-ups of local meetings appear on the front page and are referred to within other articles. Include exactly what benefit members will receive from coming to the meeting—how to cut production costs, how to manage time more efficiently, etc.

Advertising Agency:

Goal: Increase revenue by 25% this year	
Objectives:	**Strategy:**
Win two new Fortune 500 accounts.	Expand mailing list to include all Fortune 500 companies' advertising managers. Write up success stories showing other Fortune 500 accounts. Write editorials and "how to" articles showing an understanding of the special needs of these prospects.
Increase TV commercial production and placement for all clients by 10%.	Publish articles showing new equipment and services used for TV commercial production. Tell prospects why agency services produce the best advertisements. Talk about successful TV commercials in each issue.
Build franchised advertising program for car dealers.	Expand mailing list to include the targeted automotive dealerships. Create a special page inserted only in the dealers' newsletter showing the specifics of your franchised advertising program. Include statistics you've collected on how well it works. Interview other dealers using the program and use their quotes in the articles.

External Insurance Agency Newsletter:

Goal: Increase profitability	
Objectives:	**Strategy:**
Increase sales of life and disability insurance by 25%.	Write up benefits of having this type of insurance. Use testimonies to show real people who have been helped by these policies.
Maintain or decrease sales of medical coverage by 5%.	Report on the rising cost of medical coverage and the need to find a competitively-priced policy. Give readers a list of well rated, cost-effective policies. At the same time, tell readers about other types of policies and why they should buy or continue to buy these from the insurance agency.
Increase sales by 10% to small business owners within 6 months. Increase policy renewals by 25%.	Develop checklists and insurance parameters specifically for small businesses. Show through articles a good understanding of the special needs of their companies. Give readers incentives to renew their policies. Show them how you've saved them time and money over the year and how you plan to help them in the future.

Non-Profit Organization:

Goal: Increase donations & volunteer time	
Objectives:	**Strategy:**
Retain larger donors.	Make a special effort to include top donors in photographs showing fund-raising events.
Target smaller donors for $25 to $50 yearly donations.	Increase newsletter distribution by purchasing mailing lists of residents in the surrounding community. Write article detailing how donations help and requesting $25 to $50 donations.
Contact churches, scout troops and retirees in the community to recruit volunteers.	Buy list from the American Association of Retired Persons in the area. Write articles on the benefits of volunteering. Add a line to the contribution form listing the option to volunteer. Also mail the newsletter to leaders of church youth groups and scout troops. Write articles on how young people learn by volunteering.

Manufacturer:

Goal: Increase sales while decreasing seasonal fluctuations	
Objectives:	**Strategy:**
Maintain sales to existing customers.	Write articles on new products developed for existing customers. Include industry news on this market.
Have new customers accounts for 15% of sales.	Buy mailing list from a magazine or trade association serving the target market. Send newsletter showing applications of the products to the new prospects. As prospects are converted to customers, show success stories with photographs of customers using the products.

External Hospital Newsletter:

Goal: Increase community use of hospital services	
Objectives:	**Strategy:**
Increase by 15% the use of special centers such as birth unit and cancer center.	Printing success stories of patients who have overcome great difficulties by using the hospital's services.
Encourage patients to choose hospital vs. letting their doctors choose.	Tell benefits of the hospital versus those further away. Let patients know they have a choice.
Increase community use of fitness center by 10% by year-end.	Show different aspects of fitness center in each issue. Alternate focus by showing people who are older, younger, infants, athletes and recovering patients.

Employee Newsletter:

Goal: To have better-informed employees	
Objectives:	**Strategy:**
Improve employee morale and increase productivity by 15%.	Give credit to reliable, hard-working employees. Every year, list people who haven't taken sick days. Publish productivity tips submitted by employees. If an employee attends a seminar outside the company, have the person summarize the presentation. Give people information on the organization's long term and short term goals.

It's important that the specific goals of your newsletter be in line with the current short term and long term plans for your organization.

Let's look further at the specific ways your newsletter helps you achieve your promotional goals through the RISE levels. The promotional levels help you determine which newsletter elements to use to achieve your goals. For example, if you want to tell prospects about a new service you'd do one or all of the following:

R➤   place a teaser about the product on the mailing panel

I➤   show the product in a photograph along with a caption

S➤   detail the features of the product in an article

E➤   include a reply card to request information about or to order the new product or service

Your choice depends on the promotional level of your newsletter. In general, most newsletters promote at all of the levels. One recipient may only look at the return address and throw the newsletter away. Another reader of the same newsletter may read it from cover to cover and then call you for more information. On the average, your newsletter will perform at only one of the four promotional levels.

To determine which level it will be, look closely at how the following factors relate to your organization. The RISE promotional levels are used in a variety of ways depending on:

➤ how well you're known
➤ whom you're promoting to
➤ what you're promoting
➤ why they'd enlist your services or support your cause

Let's examine these factors.

Are You Familiar Territory to Your Prospects?

Look at the average characteristics of your targeted readers. The mix of customers and prospects tells you how well you are known. Your existing customers should recognize your name, along with some of your prospects. But not everyone knows you. It depends on how long you've been around and how active you've been at promoting yourself in the past.

Well-established organizations worry little about name recognition. Industry leaders like IBM can assume most of their prospects have heard of them. They are more concerned with image and distributing information.

Newcomers, however, face a different challenge. Not only do they have to gain name recognition, they often must work within a small budget. Newcomers usually give the most attention to the name recognition and image techniques. Their reader base consists primarily of prospects.

For example, a lawyer building a practice wants to become known. At first, she concentrates on recognition and image. She publishes a one-page monthly newsletter to regularly put her name on the desks of area businesses. The lawyer pays attention to the newsletter's name and the subjects covered to show expertise in certain areas. To speed up the image-building phase, she also holds legal workshops for local business associations. From working with other law firms, she knows she must convince prospects of her expertise. Potential clients must trust her before they'll give her their business. She also knows that direct sales calls are considered "unprofessional" for lawyers. The average amount of time it takes to win a new client using these marketing approaches is six to 12 months.

Two years later, the lawyer has a substantial list of clients. She changes the newsletter to a four-page quarterly and adds some photographs and a second color for highlight. The newsletter mailing list includes more clients than prospects. The articles are longer and contain more specific information on legal issues. This keeps and increases business from existing clients. Because the lawyer now has more money than time, she subcontracts the editing and production and only writes up a rough draft of the articles herself. She holds fewer workshops and relies more on word of mouth from satisfied clients. If she wants to get business from larger corporations, she concentrates on the quality of paper and printing of the newsletter to give prospects the best possible image. If she's interested in more work from small businesses, she uses recycled paper to give an approachable, practical image.

How Well You're Known	
New to my market	Recognition
Name becoming established, products or services not yet known	Image
Name, products, and services known; need way to inform and educate on features or specifics	Specifics
All information known; need more response & feedback	Enactment

From this example, you can see how your newsletter changes along with your organization's growth. You can also see how you can start out with a less expensive publication and expand the project as it proves itself.

Your mix of customers and prospects affects your promotional level the same way. You have to look at which parts of your business you're expanding. If you're branching out to a new area, prospects may be more important to reach than existing customers. Catch their attention with short articles that summarize your services. If you're concentrating on existing customers, you can give more detailed information on your services.

Choosing between promoting through image or specifics also depends on the complexity of your products and services.

Types of Products Promoted by Image & Specifics

A computer parts manufacturer sent out a newsletter with pictures and descriptions of three new products. Since there was little competition and great demand for the products at the time, it received hundreds of reply cards just by letting buyers know it had the products they needed. The design and quality of the newsletter was professional. This kept buyers from faltering on the fact they didn't recognize the company's name.

Obviously, the more complex the product, the more information people need before they choose it. As a general rule, newsletters offering specifics are good for any organization which has to educate buyers and supporters in order to promote its products and services. Image newsletters are ideal for simple products and services. Sometimes, though, there's more to the puzzle. Other pieces include competition and the rate of change within your organization.

Image newsletters are valuable for products and services which have little competition. Often, winning a supporter is just a matter of letting prospects know you have the product or service they need.

Specifics newsletters are ideal for industries with rapid changes and scarce information. By providing prospects with needed information, many organizations differentiate themselves from their competitors.

One publisher in the plastics industry uses a newsletter to keep customers and prospects informed. Even though plastics is a 50-year-old market, the pace of change is amazing. The publisher has successfully used a newsletter in combination with direct sales to inform its readers of industry changes as well as changes in its product line.

The computer industry has also been fertile ground for newsletters. Manufacturers, software producers and computer dealers are all frequent newsletter publishers. This market has solved several problems with newsletters. With daily technological breakthroughs, customers and prospects struggle for information. In addition, until computers became mainstream, few experts on the technology had the time to teach others to use the machines. Instead, new users had to sit down with complex manuals and figure out everything on their own. Meanwhile their bosses breathed down their necks to see the results showed in the brochures.

Hospitals have similar challenges to those of the computer industry. New medical technology is bringing computerized testing equipment into hospitals. Since roughly 75% of the population consider themselves wary of computers, health institutions have the challenge of informing patients of new services without scaring them away. Successful promotional newsletters show people, instead of equipment, and tell how the equipment helped them.

Image building newsletters are often shorter and easier to write. Because they don't have to provide as much information as specific newsletters, they contain less text and more photographs and illustrations. As noted in the two following examples, you can usually publish an image newsletter at a cost less than a specifics newsletter.

Some products and services can be sold through image alone, while others have to go through the longer process of explaining specific information to prospects. As an example, here are two different companies with an almost identical customer base.

Specifics Newsletter Works for Music Store

Music Man is a Nashville-area dealer of musical instruments. The store sells computerized keyboards and synthesizers, and also sponsors free clinics and product demonstrations. Before starting a newsletter, the owner had trouble keeping musicians updated on new products. Ideally, the store would mail an individual announcement for each event or new product. With a mailing list of over 5,000 names, individual mailings were cost-prohibitive. For Music Man, publishing a newsletter was an efficient way to consolidate mailings and still inform customers of new products and upcoming events in a timely fashion.

The newsletter contains product announcements accompanied by black and white photos. The editor saves press releases and orders media kits from the companies sponsoring clinics and demonstrations. With minor changes, these are turned over to a production service and put directly into newsletter format.

The newsletter also benefits from an attentive customer base. People in the music industry are open to new ideas and experimental by nature. They are also avid subscribers of magazines and like reading about applications and features of the new equipment. They also like knowing who else is using the equipment. A newsletter detailing product specifications is exactly what Music Man needs to promote its merchandise.

Night Club's Success With Image Newsletter

A business catering to virtually the same audience had a completely different

experience with a specifics newsletter. The Bluebird Cafe, also located in Nashville, is a nationally-known night club for songwriters.

To promote the cafe, the owner started publishing a bi-monthly newsletter with a calendar insert listing upcoming performances. The body of the newsletter featured interviews with some of the performers along with local music news and stories about the club.

Though feedback from the readers was positive, the owner objected to the time it took away from her staff. Unlike Music Man, they were writing original material. Putting together the body of the newsletter was taking 40 to 50 hours per issue. Also, due to the transitory nature of club musicians, the bi-monthly calendar insert would be outdated and full of changes within a few weeks.

The editor solved the problem by taking the element of the newsletter that brought people into the club—the calendar insert—and published it "solo" as a monthly flier. It also doubled as an announcement to be posted and handed out in the club. The newsletter body is still published, but only to detail special events such as the club's annual anniversary celebration. The editor successfully converted her newsletter from a specifics to an image publication without any loss of business to the club.

The promotional level for your newsletter depends on the information your prospects need before they decide to support you and how long it takes them to make a purchase decision.

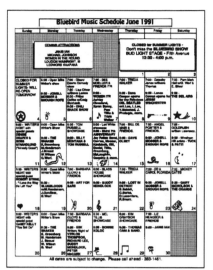

Calendar insert.

How Long it Takes to Climb Your Mountain

The complexity of your products determines the average time it takes to convert a prospect to a customer—the distance of the climb. For Music Man, most musicians were spending from $500 to several thousand dollars on equipment. They wanted to first see the product demonstrated, take a brochure home and study it, see a review, and read about it in the newsletter. This is true of industrial buyers as well. Over 90% prefer seeing some type of printed literature before they will buy.

Some services and causes also have long mountain climbs. A voter making a decision on a candidate needs time and information since the politician will hold office for several years. Most voters take their responsibility seriously. People want to know how the candidate stands on all of the major issues and they want to know about the candidate's background and perspective.

On the other hand, customers at the Bluebird Cafe are making a decision that will cost them $5 to $20. Usually the decision is made in a matter of seconds when a friend invites them along. Her image newsletter is sufficient to win a customer given her short mountain climb.

Time it Takes to Convert a Prospect	
Products purchased or support given on impulse	Recognition
Product purchased or support quickly given based on special need (little competition)	Image
Products purchased or support given only after lengthy gathering of all of the facts	Specifics
Prospects ready to act now; need to know how	Enactment

Usually, the more expensive and complex the product and long-term the relationship, the longer it takes your prospect to make a purchasing decision.

This brings us to the purchasing decision itself. The better you know your prospects, they more you can influence their decision to buy, join, donate or vote.

Why Prospects Climb Your Mountain

In order to provide information that promotes your products, services and causes, you have to know what has made people support you in the past. You also have to know their common questions or problems and why some won't buy from or support you.

The answers to these questions aren't always simple. It's also not necessarily the same for every prospect. Even so, you can spot some trends and this information helps you develop effective visuals and article content.

In Chapter 6, you'll be given methods of surveying your customers. For now, make your own estimation by looking at the ways you've been attracting customers or supporters. Music Man sent sales fliers and special event notices to current customers and advertised their sales and special events in the newspaper. Why did this work?

Why Prospects Become Supporters	
Because they've heard of your organization	Recognition
Because your organization has a good reputation	Image
Because you offer exactly what they need	Specifics
Because they were ready to respond and received the incentive to do so	Enactment

A quick guess is that the events and products advertised were of interest to their customers and prospects. Once the prospects knew that the store carried interesting items, they came in to get more information.

Many professional services such as doctors, lawyers and accountants get business through referrals. Prospects like getting a recommendation from someone else because it makes it a "safe" choice. It also saves them the time they might have to spend to find a good service. To others, it's important to know they're dealing with the same organizations as their colleagues.

People giving money to charities want to know more about the people their money will help. They also want to know that their donations will be spent effectively.

Charting Your Own Course

Concentrate on the promotional levels you need to achieve the goals of your newsletter, but keep in mind that your newsletter promotes at all levels. If an image newsletter is right for you, pay special attention to image techniques. This doesn't mean you won't provide any specifics or ways to respond. Include detailed information for those who want it. Also, provide a response mechanism—as basic as listing your phone number and store hours or as elaborate as a postage paid reply card offering a gift to respondents.

Use the form below to identify your mountain and chart the promotional path. First, list the current promotional goals for your organization. Using the previous examples, list some of the specific ways you can achieve this original goal through your newsletter.

If your goal is to find new customers, members or supporters, think about where you've been getting them so far. How can you get more from this same source? Are there other sources you think are viable? Figure out how you can find these prospects' names and addresses. Then plan out how you can attract their attention in your newsletter.

Your Current Promotional Goals:	
Your Objectives:	Your Strategy:

Studying promotional levels helps you determine what other types of promotions you should consider. For instance, some companies are concerned with establishing their reputations such as a chiropractor or a chemical company that's been under fire for environmental reasons. Since their newsletters focus on image, they need other marketing programs to help with their promotions. The chemical company uses direct salespeople and places advertisements in industry journals. The chiropractor holds workshops and attends Chamber of Commerce meetings to find patients directly. Their newsletters play an important part in their marketing programs. Carefully planning your marketing assures that you will achieve the most benefit from each tool, including your newsletter.

Part of Long-Term Marketing

Your newsletter is a vital part of your marketing plan—but it's still only a part. As already stated, basic communication theory says that the same information must be presented in four different ways before you can assume your prospect is aware of your message. While you're establishing recognition and image, giving specifics, and inviting enactment through your newsletter, you're probably simultaneously using other marketing tools that do the same thing. Make sure your newsletter works with these other projects by integrating your newsletter into the rest of your marketing plan.

A marketing manager in the computer industry used a newsletter along with other media as a standard method of introducing new products. With each new product or service, her staff would:

> send press releases to a list of 1,000 publications

> include an article in the newsletter introducing the product

> publish (in a later addition of the newsletter) a list of publications where a review of the product appeared

> send a direct mail piece to dealers and prospects

> insert an ad in the newsletter

> even later, feature a case history of the product in the newsletter

The newsletter was the backbone of the new product launch. Readers would see the product mentioned again and again in a variety of interesting ways. The repetition helped sell more of each product.

A marine parts distributor used a newsletter to help launch a new campaign designed to tell customers that it delivered parts faster than the competition. The owner developed a delivery warranty program called "Delivery Guaranteed."

Sticker.

The company placed stickers on its packaging, distributed a brochure detailing the program, instructed salespeople to tell all of their customers, and included an article in the newsletter. The newsletter article appeared first and explained the program in detail. Then, when prospects received the brochure and saw stickers on every box, they were reminded again about the benefits of the program.

Newsletter article.

Brochure.

Your marketing goals or special promotions may be enhanced using similar tools along with your newsletter. If the primary goal for your newsletter is one listed on the chart on the following page, consider using its accompanying marketing tool to reinforce the promotional efforts of your newsletter.

A newsletter should be just one of your marketing tools. Coordinate it with your other marketing plans. This way your marketing efforts will be much more effective (and at a lower cost) because each effort reinforces other efforts.

Other Marketing Tools Used Along With Newsletters

Objectives:	Supplementary Marketing Tools:
Create or enhance your image as an industry expert.	Seminars
Promote your organization's achievements and future plans to stockholders, vendors, customers, supporters and employees.	Annual Report
Give customers and prospects useful information and "how to" advice so they'll save the piece and have your organization's name in mind.	Informational Booklet
Explain how a product or service works; highlight benefits and uses.	Product or Service Brochure
Explain capabilities and philosophy of organization.	Company Brochure
Tell success stories of customers who have used your products to solve specific problems.	Case History
Provide prospects with complete list of products and services along with specific information.	Catalog
Announce sales and specials.	Circulars (Retail Stores)
Give prospects technical specifications of products.	Data or "Spec" Sheet
Provide the industry with news of new products, services or offers; inform of organization changes; reach influential or innovative people in the industry.	Public Relations
Meet customers and prospects face-to-face in one central location; give hands-on demonstrations of services.	Trade Shows and Conventions
Meet prospects in person for a one-on-one discussion of their needs and explanation of how your products or services solve them.	Direct Sales Call
Speed up response or mountain climb; qualify prospects.	Telemarketing

Editorial Calendar Coordinates Newsletter With Other Promotions

Combine your newsletter with your yearly marketing plan by creating an editorial calendar for the newsletter. Depending on how quickly your industry or organization changes, it can be difficult to plan for everything. Many events, however, are announced well in advance. Examples include seminars, annual conventions, elections, annual fund-raising events, special issues of trade magazines and new product launches. Here are some samples.

Plastics Manufacturer Selling to Various Markets

Issue:	Marketing Projects:	Newsletter Features:
Jan./Feb.	Salespeople concentrate on auto industry scale up. Direct mailing to auto makers.	Show products in auto applications. Provide "how to" information for auto designers. Report on the trends of plastic use in cars. Interview employee who specializes in auto industry.
Mar./Apr.	Salespeople concentrate on appliances & construction. Ad in an appliance magazine.	Show appliance applications for plastic. Include how plastic saved manufacturers money. List specifications of materials suggested for use. Give phone number of on-staff expert to call.
May/June	Ad in a packaging magazine. Mention in editorial.	Report on changing cooking habits of today's households. Show the role of plastics in this trend. Discuss the advantage of using the company's plastics to make cooking trays. Show analysis of cost versus top competitor. Include reply card for special report on the material.
July/Aug.	Ad in an outdoor furniture magazine. Direct mail campaign to furniture manufacturers.	Show use of plastic in outdoor chairs and tables. Show results of extensive weathering study. Interview customers and include quotes on why they use the material. Publish study of market growth for plastic furniture. Provide list of upcoming conventions and your booth numbers.
Sept./Oct.	Outdoor furniture convention. Plastics industry convention.	Provide overview of complete list of products and their potential uses. Print extra newsletters for handouts at conventions. Advise readers how to handle questions from consumers.
Nov./Dec.	Gift boxes mailed to customers. Cards mailed to prospects. Customers invited to holiday banquet.	Report on the state of the plastic industry. Discuss your plans for the upcoming year and how they will benefit customers. Include a letter thanking customers for their business.

Multiple Sclerosis Society

Issue:	Marketing Projects:	Newsletter Features:
January	Crawfish boil at local club.	Include an article encouraging the community to make pledges to cyclists for the spring fund-raising bicycle ride. Show people who have been helped through the donations to the organization. Provide more information on the bicycle ride route and schedule to increase the number of riders.
April	Spring fund drive. Spring Breakaway bike ride. Local PR and brochures for ride. Thank you letters to riders and sponsors.	Recognize top donors and top fund raisers from the bike ride. Show their pictures along with a quote on why they support the event. Recognize sponsors of the event and encourage readers to patronize these businesses.
July	July & August Monte Carlo night.	Encourage community to make pledges for fall ride. Report on the year's progress in helping people with multiple sclerosis. Tell how many riders are expected for the weekend fall ride and give more information on the events and sponsors.
October	Fall fund drive. Tour for Cure bike ride. Local PR and brochures for ride. Thank you letters to riders and sponsors.	Focus on fund-raising programs in schools. Report on fall bike ride. Include pictures of cyclists. Write an article on the top fund raiser. Include a holiday greeting for donors and fund raisers from MS patients.

As you go through the year, update the calendar to include new products and advertising campaigns. To reinforce an advertisement or direct mailing, you may even want to insert the same promotional literature into your newsletter.

When choosing the timing for your most interesting promotional material, plan around the times of year your customers usually buy, join or donate. For retailers, a Federal Reserve study showed the months of consumer spending from highest to lowest as: December, November, October, September, May, April, June, August, March, January, July and February. Look at the revenue trends for your specific organization and use them in your planning.

For example, the nursery business is seasonal. One nursery publishes a four-page newsletter once during the summer, fall and winter. The newsletters provide seasonal information such as summer watering tips, fall tree planting, and Christmas poinsettias and frost protection. Because business is best in the spring, it publishes a two-page newsletter every other week for the first two months of the spring planting season. This increased frequency keeps the nursery on the minds of its prospects who are waiting for the first sign of good weather to go out and buy some plants.

You should also consider the times when people pay more attention to direct mail. Studies by the Direct Marketing Association show that people read and respond to direct mail the most in September, October, November, January and February. It makes sense, as these are periods when vacation season is over, children are back in school and people have returned to work. These periods must trigger a "back to school" feeling in most people, regardless of age, setting an ideal climate for reading publications.

Although December is one of the lowest response months, it's the ideal time to say "thank you" to your clients and members. Many organizations plan a special message for this issue. To avoid having your publication buried under someone's mail stack over the holidays, try to get it into the reader's hands before the middle of December.

A simple greeting from all of your staff creates a friendly holiday message.

Up to this point, you've seen all of the ways newsletters can be used to promote. You know whether or not you *should* publish a newsletter. The next step is to determine if you *could* publish a promotional newsletter—whether you have the equipment and capabilities to generate the publication you need or whether you'll need to find outside help.

5

Saving Time & Money

When building your path up the mountain, you must operate within finite boundaries. There is always limited time, money and other resources. In this chapter, you'll learn how to analyze the resources of your organization to determine:

> ➤ if you can do a newsletter
> ➤ which parts of the project you'll subcontract

Regularly-published newsletters come from the organizations which planned carefully at the beginning for the time and money they could spend. Many publishers, however, start a newsletter only to cancel it when they discover the true cost both in terms of cash outlay and time involved. Just as you wouldn't start construction on a bridge without having the money for the last link, you shouldn't start a newsletter without first analyzing the costs. Make sure you have the money to publish on a regular basis.

In addition to money, consider the time it takes to do a newsletter. Many organizations underestimate this. If you're to do most of the work yourself, you have to be able to set aside large blocks of uninterrupted time. Otherwise, you'll have a half-completed newsletter sitting on your desk for months, always being pushed aside for something more immediate. Many a time-depleted self-publisher ends up working on the newsletter after dark.

To help you plan for the time, resources and money newsletters require, this chapter includes several checklists. They are designed to help you see just how much time a newsletter takes and the resources you need to do it yourself. If you find you need help, newsletter subcontractors are listed along with how to find them. Setting and stretching your budget are covered toward the end of the chapter. Lastly, you'll find out how to coordinate the job to make sure you meet time and budget estimates.

Newsletters Take Time and Other Resources

The time it takes you to produce each issue depends on how much of the work you do yourself, the amount of experience you have, and the page size, length, and frequency of your newsletter.

For all publishers, it takes two to three times as long to produce the first issue as it takes to produce subsequent ones. This is because you must set goals, create the name and design, and make all of the other initial decisions involved with publishing a newsletter.

Some of the time taken to create the first issue is spent meeting with other people. Either on your own, or in a group, sit down and:

➤ set up a rough budget
➤ determine the newsletter's promotional goals
➤ identify prospective readers
➤ discuss sources for names and addresses of these prospects
➤ decide how the mailing list will be compiled and where it will be stored
➤ develop content
➤ name your newsletter
➤ decide on the newsletter's size, format and frequency
➤ gather newsletter designs you think will work well for you
➤ decide who will design the newsletter

Use examples in this book as guidelines for these steps.

If you're working on your own or with a small group of people, it will take a week or two to finalize these decisions and feel comfortable with your choices. If you're working within a larger organization and need to receive outside approval, plan on a month or so.

Some of the initial steps require not only time, but special resources. For instance, in order to set up your own mailing list, you need access to and the ability to use a computerized database. To design your own newsletter, you need experience with design basics. If you don't have these resources, start looking for possible subcontractors.

Part of creating your newsletter includes deciding who will handle each of the following production steps as you publish each new issue of the newsletter:

> planning content
> collecting information
> finding visuals
> writing articles, headlines, captions
> editing and proofreading
> typesetting and layout
> printing labels; labeling, sorting and delivering newsletter
> following up on inquiries

Each of these steps take time. The exact amount depends on the newsletter's size and length, number of prospective readers and amount of the project you do yourself.

If you choose to learn as you go and handle all of the newsletter production yourself, set aside a few weeks to concentrate only on the newsletter. If you're using equipment for the first time, read all of the manuals. Read this book along with any other newsletter information you've collected. This saves you time in the long run. For a standard-size four-page newsletter it will take you roughly two weeks to finish the newsletter in addition to any training you need.

To give you a rough idea, if you are experienced with newsletters, research, writing, and production will take between four and five working days for a four-page newsletter with photographs. For a one-page newsletter, it takes about one working day.

These steps also require capabilities that you can learn from this book along with others such as *Editing Your Newsletter* and *Newsletters From the Desktop* listed in Appendix B. Some require special equipment. To typeset and lay out your newsletter, for example, you need minimal equipment of at least a typewriter or preferably a computer and laser printer for desktop publishing.

The best way to save time is to find help with the parts of the project you are inexperienced with. For example, don't buy a desktop publishing system and try to produce your first newsletter in a few days. Subcontract the newsletter layout while you're learning your new system. See if your subcontractor will train you once you know the basics of your system.

Using Your Own Marketing Expertise

If you have the capabilities, or are interested in cultivating them within your organization, there are advantages to building your own path up the mountain. Many editors value the knowledge they gain from working on a newsletter. It gives them opportunities to talk with customers and other important people in the industry. One editor commented that newsletter production kept her more up-to-date on the market and the needs of her clients. She was seeing the results in increased sales.

The skills developed while producing a newsletter are also useful for other marketing projects. They're so handy, it may be worth the investment of time and money to get professional training. You can attend seminars for newsletter editing, design and desktop publishing (see listing in Appendix B). To improve your writing, take a news reporting class at a community college. The skills needed to write powerful editorial copy can be used for press releases.

"We used to subcontract the writing of our newsletter. Every month, the writer would talk with industry experts, interview our clients, and pour over stacks of trade journals. As a result, she was as up-to-date as the marketing, sales, and public relations people in our firm. Through her expertise, she was able to write a successful publication for our company. Then we started to think of how her insight could help with other marketing projects. We hired her full-time."

A relatively inexpensive investment in desktop publishing equipment and training allows you to typeset and layout the newsletter yourself. With the same equipment you can produce proposals, manuals, catalogs and brochures.

If you choose to mail the newsletter yourself, you can find free supplies and information at your local post office. For more detailed rules, they can sell you a publication called the *Domestic Mail Manual*. It includes regulations for the various ways to mail, including first, second and third class.

Chances are your organization has a lot of hidden talent you can draw on to help with other steps in newsletter production. An amateur photographer can take photographs at a convention for you; an illustrator may also be able to create professional-looking cartoons. Others may be willing to proofread or help you label newsletters. The more of your own staff you involve, the greater the support and awareness of the publication within your organization.

Advantages of Subcontractors

One problem many organizations face is their lack of time, especially small businesses. In the U.S., 85% of the businesses have fewer than 20 people. These small businesses need ways to subcontract marketing tasks in order to keep their time free for day-to-day business operations.

If you have more money than time, hiring subcontractors to write and produce your newsletter might be the path to choose. Even if you're strapped for cash, you may still save money and end up with a more effective sales piece.

One of the benefits of using subcontractors is that, over time, you may get better work at lower cost than by doing it yourself. With hourly charges of $20 to $100 this may be hard to believe at first glance, but often a professional can do the same job in a fraction of the time it would take you. This frees your time for other marketing tasks, easily adding enough to your bottom line to cover the subcontractor's fee.

By using outside vendors, you relieve yourself of the everyday chores and problems involved in producing a newsletter. However, to keep the news-letter on track, you must still be involved in planning and gathering article ideas.

The best part of working with subcontractors is that they rely on regularly published newsletters for their income. This way, you have people on your production team with an incentive to complete each issue and get the next one in the works.

Services Offered by Subcontractors

Finding good subcontractors can be tricky. Ask friends and associates for suggestions. When a newsletter catches your eye, call the publisher and ask who handles the individual production tasks. Seek out local communication organizations. Look in the Yellow Pages. Or, find one vendor and let them refer you to the others. For example, your printer—especially those who print a lot of newsletters—can refer you to capable designers, newsletter specialists, typographers and mailing services.

Subcontracting your promotional newsletter production isn't an all or nothing proposition. You can match your in-house capabilities with those of the subcontractors. For example, if you have a desktop publishing system and feel comfortable doing the layout in-house, you can find independent writers to create the content. Then, you can oversee the printing and mailing yourself. If you feel comfortable with writing, you can subcontract the production.

The following is a description of how each subcontractor can help you.

Marketing consultant. A marketing consultant might be a good person to start with when setting up your newsletter project. A good consultant can help you with your newsletter project by looking at your goals and available resources, then pointing you toward other specialists for the parts of the project you're unable to do in-house. Most consultants have extensive lists of advertising agencies, freelance writers, direct mail companies, and so on, to help you with your newsletter.

Locating: The best place to find a good consultant is a referral from an organization with successful marketing. You can also look in the Yellow Pages under "marketing consultants." However, many of the listings are ad agencies who provide more than pure consultation and who may not be as objective as someone only offering information.

Public relations firm, advertising agency, or newsletter production shop. You may want to find someone who can handle everything from writing through distribution. These specialists have either internal resources or subcontractors for every step of your newsletter's production. They have already spent the time and trouble to find vendors who are reliable, affordable and quality conscious.

Locating: Look in Yellow Pages listings under "advertising" and "public relations" and see if any of the firms specify newsletters, communications, or publications in their listings. Contact professional associations for local referrals (see Appendix B). Seek referrals from printers, typesetters, desktop publishing firms, marketing consultants and mailing services.

Designer. As part of creating your first issue, an experienced designer can help you produce a newsletter with a professional image. The artist can design your nameplate, page design, color combinations, typefaces, and any other graphic elements used to make the newsletter inviting to read.

If you plan to use desktop publishing equipment for the layout, some designers will provide the template in electronic format. If not, you or your desktop publishing service can turn a sketch into a template.

> "At first, I designed our newsletter. Since I'm a writer not a designer, our first year's volume of newsletters had a hodgepodge of looks—not exactly the way to build recognition!
> Luckily, we found a good designer. This artist designed a newsletter we liked and put it in a Page-Maker format for my Macintosh. Each issue, I just placed the text and graphics on the page. The newsletter looks great and the money we spent is much less than the time I was spending fiddling with the design."

Locating: Advertising agencies have lists of independent designers they may share with you. Designers can also be referred by freelance writers, marketing consultants, printers, mailing services, or typesetting service. In the Yellow Pages, designers are listed under "artists–commercial."

List management service. If you don't have the equipment and personnel to set up and maintain your own mailing list, consider a list management service. This service sets up your mailing list on their computers and can add, remove, and change addresses and other information to your list. The advantage of list management services is that they already have the database structures and can set up a sophisticated list with much more information than just the mailing address. The disadvantage is that you may want to have the ability to access customer, donor, or member information from your own office.

If you decide to use this service, look for one which can update and transfer the list to the system you use. If you also need a service for labeling your newsletters, find one that also provides list storage and maintenance. Many do.

Locating: Look in the Yellow Pages under "mailing list management." List management services are also handled by mailing services and secretarial services.

Writer. Once you set up the newsletter design and mailing list, you'll develop the content for the first issue. Then, either you or someone else needs to collect the information needed to write the articles. Professional writers are able to research and write your newsletter. They understand how to collect information and turn it into attention-getting copy needed to draw readers into an article.

For best results, find a writer with experience in your particular industry. A writer familiar with banks, for example, knows the jargon and how the industry works. These writers require less briefing and offer you fresh suggestions by bringing you experience from businesses similar to yours.

You can give your writer a general outline of a story assignment and she will write it, or you can give her rough notes or first draft and she will rework it into a professional piece. If you're new to writing, a writer can edit your articles for you and, through this process, you can improve your writing.

Locating: Newspapers, magazines, local tabloids, and advertising agencies all use independent writers. Most publications are willing to pass along some names. You can also find newsletter writers by asking designers, desktop publishing services, marketing consultants, printers, and typesetting services. In the Yellow Pages, look under "editorial services" or "writers."

Desktop publishing service. There are several ways to get the words you have written into a page format. One method is with a desktop publishing service. Using microcomputers and laser printers, these services take your typed newsletter content and newsletter design and do your newsletter layout at a reasonable price. For high-quality promotional newsletters, their work can be output on high resolution typesetting equipment. Many desktop publishing services will also design your newsletter.

Locating: Look in the Yellow Pages under "desktop publishing" and also under "typsetting." These services may also be found through printers, writers, marketing consultants and mailing services.

Typesetting service. Typesetters use sophisticated equipment to format the words you have written and output them in a desired typestyle, size and column width. With the boom of microcomputers into electronic publishing, many typesetting services can output your type in page layout form. Those using the old method will give you the type in columns (called "galleys") and may also provide a pasteup service to paste the galleys onto a design board.

> "I always thought that most people only noticed my news-letter's design and layout. I knew it was important to proofread but I didn't always have the time. Then, one day my boss brought in a copy of the newsletter that had been returned by our best donor. All of the errors were highlighted in yellow. The page looked like a canary shed on it! I added a proofreader to my production team on the next issue."

You can submit your newsletter articles to them either on paper, which requires rekeying, or on computer disk.

Locating: Look in the Yellow Pages under "typographers." Also seek referrals from designers, writers and printers.

Proofreader. These eagle-eyed readers scrutinize your final layout for misspelled words, grammatical errors, and other errors. If you're writing the newsletter yourself, you can increase overall quality by hiring a professional or finding a skilled volunteer to proofread your work.

The need for proofreading can't be stressed enough. You're striving to produce a professional-looking newsletter. Nothing adds to professionalism more than accurate facts, perfect spelling and proper grammar.

Locating: Some writers also provide proofreading services. Another source of proofreaders is through your typesetter or desktop publishing service. To find volunteers, look for detail-oriented people who are meticulous in their work.

Service bureau. If you produce your own newsletter using a desktop publishing system, consider having the final output printed from typesetting equipment versus a laser printer. The type and scanned photographs can be printed at a higher resolution and look better than those from a laser printer. However, high-quality laser printers are available that approach the quality of typesetting equipment. Though they are more expensive, consider them when purchasing a new laser printer.

Locating: Look under "typesetting" in the Yellow Pages and see if there are services with software and equipment compatible with yours. Call your local computer users' group and ask about service bureaus in the area.

Printer. Your printer is one of your most important subcontractors. Though it's tempting to choose a printer based on price only, quality, turnaround time, and service will affect your overall "price" as much as the actual bottom line. This is because poor printing quality will hurt your image, slow turnaround affects your schedule, and poor service causes you to spend more of your time coordinating the project. The wrong printer could make your newsletter take much longer than necessary to produce.

To save up to four hours per issue, find a printer that has full time salespeople. Your salesperson keeps track of when your newsletter should arrive, remembers to follow up on any problems, and picks up and delivers artwork, proofs and finished printing. Since it will otherwise be up to you to handle these tasks, the extra expense (if any) is usually well worth the time you save.

Make sure to gather several bids when you begin your newsletter project. Along with requesting firm prices, request a guaranteed turnaround time. Choose a printer who is set up to provide rapid service and who understands the timely nature of a newsletter.

After the printer has produced one of your newsletters, and assuming you're happy with the work, negotiate a yearly printing contract. Yearly contracts can cut your printing bill by up to 30%.

If you use desktop publishing to produce your newsletter, look for a printer who can take your disk and print it out on their typesetting equipment. This saves you time by not having to take your disk to a service bureau first. Many experts predict that soon your printer will be able to take

"I thought I was so shrewd. One day a man called on me and gave me a great price on my newsletter—almost 50% less than I was paying. I gave him my next newsletter job. When he didn't show up on the day it was due, I called the print shop. It turns out, this man was an independent rep and they hadn't seen him in a few days. They knew nothing about my job. It took days to get my artwork back. I took it to my tried and true printer. The issue was two weeks late. I questioned low prices from then on."

your computer file and make printing plates directly without having a printout on paper or film.

Many printers can also address and mail out your newsletter. Some have ink jet printing capabilities that access database information and address your newsletters automatically. These same capabilities can be used to add personalized messages within the newsletter.

Locating: Seek the referral of a designer, desktop publishing service, writer, newsletter editor, mailing service, marketing consultant, advertising agency, local business or typesetting service. Consult the Yellow Pages under "printers."

Photocopy service or quick printer. For simple designs, you can use standard photocopying machines to duplicate your newsletter onto standard paper or pre-printed letterhead. If your list has only a few hundred names, the quality and price may be just right for you. Some copy services also have printing presses for higher quantity jobs.

Locating: As quality may vary, ask for a referral from a designer, desktop publishing service, writer or typesetting service. Since there are usually several in each town, look for one convenient to your office. Also check the Yellow Pages under "copying services."

> "Printing out our 5,000 name mailing list every month tied up our printer, made a lot of noise, and required someone to monitor the process. While visiting us one day, our mailing service representative suggested that he take over that part of the operation. Since the service could take our list and print the names on cheshire labels (which could be affixed using automated equipment) our mailing prices went down."

Mailing service (also called a lettershop). Once your newsletter is printed, it must quickly get into the mail. If you're short on volunteers or if you have more than 200 names on your list, it is normally worth the expense to contract a mailing service. A mailing service will affix labels and postage onto your printed newsletter, sort the pieces into zip code order, and deliver them to the post office. A good mailing service can advise you on the most cost-effective methods of mailing.

Some mailing services have the ability to take the list you have on your own system and print it out when provided a disk or when you send the information via modem. This can free up your computer's printer and may not add much to your mailing bill.

Many mailing services have printing presses. If your newsletter isn't too complicated, your mailing service may be able to print it for you.

Locating: Mailing services can be referred by designers, desktop publishing services, writers, list management services, marketing consultants, advertising agencies, printers and typesetters. Look in the Yellow Pages under "mailing services."

Once you decide on your need for any of the above subcontractors, carefully select the best available service. Remember that it takes time to orient subcontractors to you, your newsletter, organization and industry. Before you invest this time, take special care to choose the right vendors. Once you get them going, you'll spend decreasing amounts of time on each project.

To help you make a better choice, a seven step procedure for selecting subcontractors is given in Appendix A.

Finding Volunteers

For many non-profit organizations, hiring subcontractors is too expensive. Rather than finding inexperienced volunteers, ask professional services for service—as opposed to cash—donations. Depending on the extent of your newsletter's distribution, a mention in the masthead may be an excellent advertising source for newsletter vendors.

To find volunteers, try sending a special mailing to printers, editors and designers soliciting help. Follow it up with phone calls. Be sure to give full information on your organization just as you would to any other potential donor. You may be surprised at the support you get for your efforts.

Be prepared to give volunteer subcontractors some extra turnaround time but don't lower your quality standards. You want a piece that everyone will be proud of. Follow the same steps suggested for hiring paid subcontractors listed in Appendix A.

> "I extended the budget for my non-profit organization's newsletter by finding a paper distributor to donate all of the paper for our newsletter. The distributor gives us the leftovers from the large rolls. Not all of the paper matches exactly, but the newsletters are never seen side by side and, on their own, they look great."

Costs to Consider

The costs of publishing a newsletter can be broken down into one-time fees, on-going fees, and costs for producing extras such as inserts and reply cards.

Set Up Costs. Your investment of time and money will peak when you first set up your newsletter. You will be going through some of the planning discussed in the previous section and may even be going to the expense of hiring professionals to create the design for the newsletter. These initial set-up costs can include:

> ➤ consulting fees
> ➤ newsletter design
> ➤ mailing list set-up

Once you've decided the steps you'll subcontract and have chosen your vendors, collect firm quotes for each step.

Ongoing Costs. Once your newsletter is underway, you'll have the same expenses for each issue. These may include:

> ➤ writing
> ➤ photography
> ➤ photo development
> ➤ illustrations
> ➤ scans, halftones or photostats
> ➤ typing or typesetting
> ➤ layout
> ➤ typeset-quality output
> ➤ color separations if printing 4-color photographs
> ➤ newsletter printing
> ➤ domestic postage
> ➤ foreign postage (if any)
> ➤ phone calls
> ➤ mailing list maintenance
> ➤ rush charges
> ➤ tax

Other costs such as printing a year's worth of envelopes or fees for bulk rate permits and business reply numbers will be incurred yearly.

Inserts and Response Cards. If you choose to insert an advertising piece or a reply card, budget for the additional costs. Include the cost of printing, additional mail house charges for insertion, additional writing and design, and the return postage if you use business reply mail.

As you are budgeting and looking for ways to cut costs, keep the following concepts in mind.

Some costs are independent of the quantity you print and mail. These are fixed fees such as subcontractors' charges and production supplies. These fees are the same no matter how many newsletters you print. If you were to assign these fees as costs per newsletter, the cost per piece would decrease as you printed more newsletters. Printing charges aren't fixed. However, most printers charge you less per piece for 2,000 newsletters than for 200, for example. Other costs, such as postage, are fixed per piece and are independent of the number you mail.

Set up your newsletter's budget before you begin. This assures that you know what you're getting into and can make changes before the first bill comes.

Ways to Save Money

For many organizations, support from sponsors and advertising sales work to stretch a newsletter budget. For non-profit organizations, the work of volunteers and donations by services such as printers can greatly offset the costs of publishing. Some non-profit organizations are able to find sponsors to donate the cost of producing an entire issue.

Retail businesses such as book stores, for example, often have advertising money available from the manufacturers of the products they sell. A newsletter might qualify for these funds. Before relying on the assistance of your suppliers, send them a proposal along with a sample of your newsletter. Show how you want to present their products or services. Be specific about the financial support you are seeking from the supplier. Make an offer and send a contract.

Some newsletter publishers sell small advertisements to offset costs. Unless these ads are perceived as a service to readers, such as sources for hard-to-find supplies, paid advertising will water down your newsletter's image as a tightly packaged bundle of information. Ads may make your newsletter look like a magazine or newspaper.

A regional bank decided it needed a newsletter and called in its advertising agency. Without budgeting the project, they went through design after design. They drew artwork for each article, extensively rewrote all copy, and printed the newsletter on an over-sized heavy paper. The result: a bill that averaged $14 a newsletter!

The editor quickly regrouped. He decided articles would be first written up by the bank, then given to the agency for final editing. The newsletter was reduced to a standard size and the paper changed to a commonly stocked grade. They used the same creative elements, but made other changes that reduced the cost per newsletter to under $1.

An alternative to advertising is to locate a sponsor for all or part of your newsletter. For example, a financial consulting firm was able to underwrite most of the cost of its newsletter by charging a sponsorship fee. Various securities firms paid to publish informative articles on their products. The publishers achieved their goals while reducing their expenses, since the information in the articles was precisely what the firm wanted to provide its customers.

What about charging for your newsletter?

Although subscription fees may help offset the costs of publishing a newsletter, they will also discourage readership and reduce the goodwill generated by a promotional newsletter. With a free newsletter, you can change or discontinue with minimum repercussions. It's different when you've collected money from subscribers.

On the other hand, one reason for charging a nominal fee is to offset the stigma of being pure advertising matter. To some audiences, a free newsletter implies the content is worthless. Charging for the newsletter, on the other hand, implies value. If your readers think this way, be creative. Give your free newsletter apparent value by printing a per issue price on the cover or an annual subscription price in the masthead.

Some newsletters start as free publications and grow into profit centers. A consultant launched a business brokerage newsletter to help market his services. The newsletter became so successful that he began to charge a subscription fee for it and soon gave up his other business to work full time on the newsletter. Many associations start free publications which turn into subscription pieces. *Psychology Today* is such a publication. In other words, if you have something valuable to say, many people will pay for it.

Other Cost Savings

Sales Tax.   Non-profit organizations should apply for tax-exempt status to avoid being charged tax.

Mailing Permits. You can avoid paying yearly permit fees by using the services of a mail house. Some will let you print their number on your pieces as long as you use their services to handle the mail.

Postage Costs. If you regularly send other information to your mailing list, consider adding your newsletter to the mailing. This is called "piggybacking."

Rush Fees. When using subcontractors, you may be faced with rush charges if you cause the project to fall behind schedule. With careful planning and scheduling you can avoid these fees.

Subcontractor Fees. Subcontractor fees can be reduced by minimizing the time your project takes. Give subcontractors work in the most final form you can. For example, if you have written your articles on your computer system, submit the articles to your typesetter or layout service on disk. This will save them time in rekeying the text and save you money. If you know exactly how you want an article structured, provide your writer with rough notes or a draft. The same goes when working with an artist. If you know what type of illustration you want, give your artist a sketch or an example. Since most subcontractors charge by the hour, cutting time saves you money.

Involve your subcontractors in your cost reduction programs. They know best how you can save money.

Bulk Mailing. Depending on the timeliness of the information and the size of the mailing list, promotional newsletters can be mailed bulk rate. The advantage is a savings of 33% over first class. Non-profit organizations can qualify for even greater discounts. The disadvantages are that the mail must be prepared according to specific post office rules and delivery can take a lot longer. By regulation, the post office has up to three weeks to deliver this mail.

The main pitfall of bulk mailing is that many postal regulations are left to the interpretation of local officials. To avoid potential problems, work with the post office from the start. Get a signed approval for your newsletter's design and keep it on file. Check on regulations, busy times, and any other possible pitfalls. Check your design again before printing—this is your last chance to make economical changes to an improper design. If you can't make bulk mail arrangements with a minimum of fuss, consider mailing first class.

Keep Pieces Under One Ounce. One important design note: for first class mailings, unlike bulk mailings, you pay by the ounce, so you may want to design your newsletter to weigh under an ounce. Be sure to include the weight of an envelope if used. Bulk mail pieces can weigh up to 3.3667 ounces without additional charges. If the pieces weigh more, the mailing goes to a per pound rate.

Start Out Small if Money is Tight

Any size budget can be used to produce a promotional newsletter. The trick is to determine what you want and what you can afford. A newsletter can be as simple as a typewritten publication on your letterhead or as formal as a four-color publication that looks almost like a magazine.

If you're on a tight budget, the key is to start out simple. At the beginning, all it takes is access to a writer/editor, typewriter and copier. As the project proves itself, you can expand to typesetting, professional graphics and more expensive printing.

Keep in mind, though, that spending more money is not always the best way to guarantee effectiveness. Often the most effective newsletters are the more simple and straightforward.

Look at *Rita's Report.* This is a level at which almost anyone can do a newsletter. The monthly one-page, two-sided newsletter costs its publisher only $40 to print and mail 100 copies. The important thing is that it works just as well as a more expensive newsletter. As part of leafing through their mail, Rita's customers can pause for three minutes to read the investment newsletter. The newsletter offers ideas for investments and has resulted in increased business for its publisher.

The nameplate is pre-printed in burgundy ink on white offset paper. The text for each issue is printed using a laser printer and photocopied onto the pre-printed sheets with the burgundy nameplate. The reverse side of the newsletter includes the return address, masthead and other small items. The publication is folded down to letter size and mailed as a self-mailer.

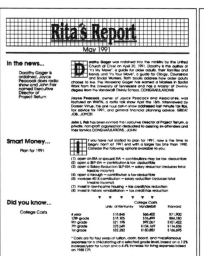
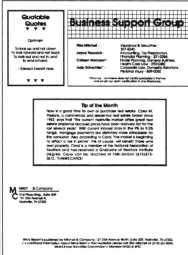

A marketing consultant uses a newsletter to promote the group's products and services. The newsletter is a legal size, one-page, two-sided mailer; the bottom section serves as a tear away reply card. The consultant pays only 50¢ each, including mailing. (The reply card requires the respondent to add a stamp.) The brevity of the articles and the helpful information keeps readers looking forward to receiving the newsletter and has also caused many to respond to its offers. The project more than funds itself from respondents' purchases and also helps with the firm's long-term marketing plans.

Of course, the frequency and length of your publication will greatly affect the yearly budget. These choices tie in to your overall marketing goals.

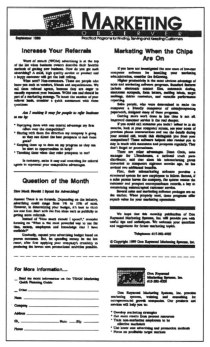

Effects of Frequency & Length on Your Budget

The general rule for frequency and length is to be brief and mail frequently. As with any type of advertising, repetition is important. A short newsletter sent once a month is preferable to a long one every quarter.

Another benefit to keeping your newsletter short is increased readership. Readership decreases as length increases. This is probably because people throw lengthy publications in their "to be read" stacks, along with magazines and long reports. If you have such a stack, you know you don't always get around to reading everything. A better approach is to send a newsletter short enough for readers to look through as they are opening their mail. If you send a one- to four-page newsletter, chances are better that most people will read at least *some* of it.

The same logic applies to using a four-page tabloid sized newsletter versus an eight-page standard size. The tabloid "looks" shorter and is easier to skim while opening the mail. At the same time, you can fit in the same amount of information as in an eight-page newsletter and, in some cases, the printing costs are equal. However, the tabloid size is more difficult to file and retrieve.

> "A newsletter should be long enough to say what you need to say and short enough to be read on the way to the wastebasket." — Mark Beach

In addition, the more frequently the newsletter comes out, the more timely the information. If your company or industry is prone to rapid change, you could have problems using a quarterly publication as a news source. If a major change takes place, it could be three months before you can get the news to your readers.

One solution is to use "special editions." Special editions are usually devoted to one topic. Occasions for special editions include trade shows, major changes, seminars or a special new product launch. The less frequently your newsletter is published, the more useful special editions can be.

Use the same design for the special edition as you do for your regular newsletter. Give readers the feeling of receiving something special by using the words "special edition," "news flash," or something similar added to the mailing panel or to the nameplate.

Whether your targeted publication schedule is quarterly, monthly or weekly, try to publish your newsletter on a regular basis. Some people know from the beginning, though, that they may have trouble with regular production.

Does haphazardness in your publication schedule show a lack of commitment to your readers? Will an irregularly published newsletter hurt rather than help your image?

I've never known anyone to be hurt by publishing just one promotional newsletter. Even if they only published their message once, they got the attention of some of their readers. The disadvantage is that they didn't stick with the project long enough to reap the benefits of longevity.

Publish your newsletter at least quarterly and preferably bi-monthly or monthly. If you feel unable to make a commitment to regular publication, admit it. A book store describes its publication, on its nameplate, as "An occasional publication of Village Books."

While publishing on a regular basis requires greater resources, you'll see the results faster. Every issue builds on the marketing efforts of the last newsletter. Within reason, the more issues your prospects see, the greater the promotional effects.

Sometimes you just may not have enough information to fill an entire issue. If not, run a smaller issue. If this happens often, you may want to publish less frequently or re-evaluate the size of the newsletter. Some organizations publish a newsletter only when they have special news or enough new product information to warrant the cost.

Information, time and costs are factors in determining the frequency and length of your newsletter. If it comes down to a choice of frequency or length, it's usually best to publish more frequently, whether this means only publishing one typewritten page, using internal staff, or cutting down on paper quality and photographs.

The best way to ensure fast turnaround on your newsletter and increase your chance of publishing on a regular basis is through developing a schedule. The schedule helps eliminate surprises by letting vendors and editorial board members know when the work is coming. Careful planning also saves you time and money.

Scheduling Your Newsletter

The most vital planning tool is the schedule you set for each issue. Developing and sticking to your schedule not only helps increase the quality of your publication, it saves you time and makes it easy to meet deadlines. You will have time to proofread, lay out and check proofs. These crucial steps are often bypassed or rushed when articles and other content are late.

For fastest turnaround, supply all of your subcontractors with a copy of your schedule and then stick to it. If you don't provide a fixed schedule, don't expect the vendor to drop other work to meet your deadline when suddenly you're in a hurry.

From a promotional viewpoint, your schedule is used to implement your editorial calendar and your marketing plan. Use your plans set in the last chapter and combine them into your scheduling.

Scheduling Your First Issue. Scheduling your first issue is somewhat of a shot in the dark. If you haven't produced a promotional newsletter before, it's hard to know how much time each step will take.

To get started, look at the steps listed on pages 50 and 51. Note the turnaround times quoted by your subcontractors or volunteers. (If timing is crucial, you may want to shop for writers, printers and mail houses for turnaround time as well as pricing.) Allow extra time for articles to be approved or other clearances your publication may require.

Next to each step, write down the estimated completion time. For your first issue, multiply this time by two.

Use this list and estimated schedule to prepare a calendar. As you complete each production stage, pencil it in on the calendar. Note any forgotten steps or discrepancies in time estimates and save the calendar to make your next schedule more accurate.

Re-adjust your schedule to keep it realistic if your newsletter misses deadlines. If the schedule can't be changed, don't expect outside services to make up for your delays without increases. Also realize that if they don't charge you more, you're still paying a price. The next time you give your vendor a schedule, they may not budget time for you until they actually receive your materials.

Letting Go of the First Issue. Although not without reward, the production of your first issue can be grueling. One editor produced his first newsletter on a new desktop publishing system under a tight schedule. The 16-page newsletter was written and produced in five days in order to distribute it at a computer industry trade show. Still feeling exhausted, the editor met a former editor of *Time* magazine at the show. He asked how *Time* was produced under a weekly deadline.

Time's editor said that it was simple. "You just learn when to let one go and always try to make the next one better."

With this in mind, publish the first issue of your newsletter as soon as possible. Once you've proofread carefully and checked that you've eliminated any major errors, send it to the printer. Don't wait until everything else is perfect. You can refine the publication along the way. It's better to publish a slightly imperfect newsletter regularly than a flawless one erratically.

Scheduling Additional Issues. When scheduling your next edition, start by evaluating the appearance and writing of your last one. Look at it critically. What was good about it? What do you think you could do to improve it? Carefully check the quality of the printing. Look at the condition of the piece after going through the postal service (be sure to add your name to your mailing list). See if the address label was put on straight. Read each article for clarity and completeness. Look at the layout and the overall design.

List the articles and important news that you want to include this time. If you have regular features—market briefs, an editorial, personnel or member profiles—include them in your list. Decide who is going to be responsible for each article and set the deadlines. Once you have your schedule, post it close by. If you check off each item when it is completed, you'll be able to spot any potential bottlenecks.

Try to avoid unpleasant surprises. Make sure the people who approve copy are going to be available when needed and those scheduled to be interviewed are still available. If possible, have backups for all vital functions and spaces. Check vacation, trade show and travel schedules. Carefully note holidays and make sure to mark them on your schedule. There's nothing worse than having everything ready for approval or preparing to interview someone, only to find that they've gone to Europe for three weeks or left early for the holidays. It has happened to the best of editors, but it doesn't need to happen to you.

If you're announcing a special event in your publication, the newsletter should arrive no earlier than four to six weeks prior to the event and no later than one week before. Regularly scheduled events such as monthly meetings should be announced no earlier than two weeks prior to the event.

Scheduling each issue can be simplified by developing a yearly editorial calendar with the help of your editorial board. By planning most of your content a year in advance, you can benefit from the economies of scale. When planning the content for upcoming issues, you only need the board's feedback for breaking news or unanticipated topics.

A yearly schedule can also save your time. Often, when you're researching one topic, you find information on a future topic as well. Rather than having to retrace your steps next time, you'll have the information on file.

From the last two chapters, you should be developing an idea of what you want your newsletter to accomplish. But in order for it to meet your goals, it has to meet the needs of your readers. Just as you have analyzed your own needs, you must also study those of your customers and prospects.

6
Scouting Out Readers' Interests

Scouting out your readers' likes and dislikes is the only way to give readers the news they want. Evaluate reader feedback and use it to guide readers on your tour up the mountain.

The first step on your scouting mission is to find out what's already available. Your trade association or an industry magazine should have demographic data such as age, sex and buying authority for your particular audience. Your fund raisers may already know the top five reasons why people support your cause. Even if a formal survey hasn't been performed, top promoters can give you a general idea. This may be all you need. Your marketing department may know the publications people read. Coordinate with the past efforts of other scouts.

Once you find out what's available and what's not, concentrate next on whether or not you need to conduct a survey. Surveys are useful for helping you develop your newsletter as well as making changes as you go along.

Surveys for new publications help you:

> find out what people want to read in your newsletter
> generate more information on your prospective readers
> see who wants to receive the publication
> find out what newsletters they're already receiving
> develop your promotional material
> justify the project to management
> assure accurate mailing addresses

Readership surveys for existing newsletters tell you:

➤ the changes readers want
➤ which parts of the newsletter are most popular
➤ who wants to continue receiving the publication
➤ how to fine-tune your promotional material
➤ whether or not your newsletter is worth its budget
➤ if your mailing list is current
➤ if your newsletter is a success

The type of survey you need depends on the accuracy of information you want. Many surveys are conducted to get a general sense of people's feelings. Numerical precision may not be a great concern. For example, you can send a response card to find out if a prospect wants to receive your newsletter.

After you've been publishing for awhile, find out if the recipients are reading your newsletter. Through this survey, give readers a forum to request the changes they want. At a minimum, send a yearly reply card asking if addresses are current and if readers want to continue receiving the publication.

One way of collecting this information is to require readers to provide it before adding their name to your list. An office products dealer does this by asking readers to check off items such as their primary type of business, title, number of employees, and types of office equipment they use. This helps the company determine how good of a prospect the reader is. It also aids in choosing the types of articles to include.

Your survey can be conducted in person, over the telephone, through a self-administered written questionnaire, or through a survey administered by an outside consulting firm. If a high response rate is important, follow-up methods like letters, incentives, reminder cards and phone calls can be used. These are proven methods for collecting statistically-accurate information.

Remember that your scouting can be done at many different levels. Readership surveys can be as informal as calling a few readers from time to time, or as formal as embarking on a full-scale research effort.

Scouting Before You Publish a Newsletter

Preliminary scouting can be used either for newsletters not yet launched or for new editors. The purpose of this scouting is to collect general information about your readers and find out what they'd read. Also, ask questions that help you qualify prospects. If you're new to your organization and industry, this knowledge is vital to your success as an editor.

You need a general idea of who your readers are—their everyday concerns, what makes them laugh, and so on. It's only through this familiarity that you can guide them through your promotional tour.

Facts like readers' age, education, sex and title determine how you will present your information in your newsletter. For example, hospital surveys have shown that women are more likely to seek health information than men. Men, however, are more likely to make an appointment with a doctor based on a newsletter article. Knowing the gender mix of its audiences, health newsletter publishers concentrate on motivating prospects to either read or respond. Or, perhaps the hospital is promoting its women's pavilion and may only want to send the newsletter to women.

Age can also affect your readership. If you are trying to attract younger people, for example, they're conditioned to the visual messages of television. They demand larger visuals and shorter blocks of text.

Sensitivity can be a problem when asking demographic questions. If you ask your readers about their marital status or age, you may often find the question unanswered. Or, you may receive the comment, "None of your business." If this information is truly important to your promotions, look at other ways to ask it. Leave it in broad enough categories so the respondent doesn't feel classified into a certain group or tempted to lie for other reasons. Respect the respondent's sensitivities and assure that answers are kept confidential.

If promoting to companies, ask for your prospect's title. From this you can determine what type of information readers require—technical, managerial, etc. You may also be able to determine their buying authority. It's dangerous to assume authority based on title alone, though. It's better to directly ask about buying authority. Unless the prospective reader is a networking contact, the person should at least influence the decision to buy from or support your organization before being added to the list.

Some people are more active readers than others. One way to spot active readers is to ask how they currently seek out information. If they read other journals or newsletters, they'll probably read your newsletter. On the other hand, if your prospects prefer going to conferences, talking with colleagues, or watching educational videos and listening to cassette tapes, you may want to explore alternatives to printed newsletters.

Once you find out how prospects receive their information, consider subscribing to the publications or attending the events your readers list. This gives you sources of information for newsletter articles that have a better chance of interesting your readers.

Useful data on your readers' organization include number of employees, industry, and type of equipment they own or are considering for purchase. This information also helps you when renting mailing lists. If you find a large number of your prospects involved in a particular industry, for example, you could rent a mailing list of that industry. Then, you could select only the portion with the common title you've found from readers.

The following questions are helpful when using the survey as part of qualifying new names for your list. Depending on the list you're using, much of this information may already be known. It may be part of the records of your sales, marketing, or fund raising departments.

?   Name (or staple business card)

?   Title

?   Are you responsible for purchasing (your product) /donating to/signing up members within your organization?
     [ ] yes
     [ ] partially
     [ ] influence
     [ ] no

?   Type of organization

?   Type of equipment owned

?   What other sources do you use for information?
     [ ] trade newspapers
     [ ] magazines
     [ ] newsletters
     [ ] trade shows
     [ ] talk with colleagues
     [ ] belong to professional groups
     [ ] conferences & trade shows
     [ ] training videos
     [ ] instructional cassette tapes
     [ ] books
     [ ] other _____

?   What are your two favorite industry magazines?
     1. _____
     2. _____

Evaluating Your On-Going Newsletter Project

Every newsletter has a goal. It could be to draw people to association activities, create new business opportunities or woo new donors. At some point, you'll need to justify to yourself and others that the project is worth the money you've budgeted. Like other marketing efforts, though, effects such as image, communication and feeling like part of the team are difficult to measure. They don't immediately appear on the bottom line. But you can still measure readers' overall response to your newsletter and awareness of its content.

The major difference between a pre-publication survey and an existing newsletter survey is now you have a newsletter to ask about. Use this survey to generate new content ideas, measure sales effectiveness, or, perhaps, as part of justifying your newsletter budget.

Although you can include a reply card in every issue, it will have limited space to initiate reader feedback. People may also tire of sending them back. As an alternative, initiate feedback from people who have the most contact with your readers. For example, you may want to ask salespeople whether they have heard comments on the newsletter. Don't underestimate informal methods. A person who has worked successfully for many years in an area, or spent hours face-to-face with your supporters, has knowledge that no survey in the world can assess. On the other hand, if you wait for feedback, you may never get it. Instead, use a formal readership survey and solicit all types of responses.

Every two to three years, conduct a readership survey. The survey lets you know what readers have been enjoying in the past issues. It can also provide you with new ideas to keep your publication fresh and interesting.

It's important to find out how much of the newsletter is read by the recipients and why they're reading it. In other words, you need to know the characteristics that differentiate *readers* from *recipients*. You can also use a survey to assess the perceived value of the information in the newsletter and measure the effect it has had on achieving the goals you've set.

The first step in asking these questions is to review your newsletter's goals and the ways you've set to achieve them.

Often, reader characteristics change due to something that happened in your industry, business or association. For example, an investment firm included a survey in its newsletter to find out how Blue Monday had affected its readers' investment attitudes. The firm found that readers had been scared by the sudden drop in stock prices. The editor adjusted the content to include articles that reassured readers and presented some more conservative investment strategies.

If one of the goals of your newsletter is "increased membership," your measure of success would be a count of new members. If the purpose were "to draw increased business from an area," the outcome measure would be amount of sales from that area. An alumnus newsletter could keep a tally of additional donations.

You can divide your goals into *short-term* and *long-term* goals. As a hypothetical example, consider the case of Acme Microchips. Acme ran into some bad times because of a glut in the microchip market. The company developed a newsletter to draw more clients. Before designing it, the staff decided on an overall goal of increased sales.

For Acme's purposes, though, the actual selling is done by a sales call to the prospective buyer. The newsletter does not sell, but creates awareness. Therefore, the purpose of the newsletter was not *long-term* (increased sales) but *short-term* (increased leads). To measure the successfulness of the newsletter, a count of the number of calls directly attributable to the newsletter was tracked. The company knows the newsletter's *purpose* and the way to measure its *outcome*.

With measurable goals, you can evaluate the success of your newsletter without a survey. Then, if you want to measure other aspects of your newsletter, you can conduct a readership survey.

Designing a Formal Survey

Formal surveys can be used to evaluate an ongoing publication or to scout out readers for a new one. For either one, ask yourself three questions when designing your survey:

> ➤ whom am I going to survey?
> ➤ what am I going to ask?
> ➤ how am I going to ask it?

When designing your survey, balance your desire for the ideal survey with cost, convenience, space and time. You must decide between written surveys, telephone surveys, personal interviews or focus groups. For example, if you decide to mail a written survey, you can survey a large number of people, but you can't ensure a large response. People don't enjoy filling out long questionnaires. On the other hand, a focus group survey allows you to ask more in-depth questions but to fewer people.

Selecting Your "Sample"

The Census, sponsored every 10 years by the U.S. government, is one of the few surveys in which (ideally) all of a given population is surveyed. Most surveys select a portion of a group to be studied and survey only this "sample." After the sample is chosen, everything possible is done to elicit responses.

This is contrary to most marketing campaigns in which a mailing is sent to a large list. These campaigns usually get a zero to five percent response rate from the people who attend meetings, speak loudest, volunteer to respond, or are convenient to poll. You're not reaching the people who don't support you. And these people may have something valuable to tell you.

The best type of sample is a random sample, which means everyone in your entire readership has a chance of being selected. For readership surveys, organizations with elaborate computer database programs can run a function in which the computer selects a given number of names at random. For simpler systems, printing out your mailing list by alphabetical order and selecting every fifth name, for example, is one method. Or, if you have 1,000 names and want 100 for a sample, select every tenth name.

Your choice of sample size ultimately boils down to the amount of money and time you have to conduct the sample. A basic rule is this: the larger the sample the more reliable the results. Also, the smaller your readership base, the higher percentage you want to sample. If you're conducting a telephone survey, you won't be able to contact as many as you would if mailing out a written survey. Choose the number based on the time you have. Then, strive for a response from every person in your sample.

Generating a 100 percent response rate from a selected sample is much more accurate than a five percent response from the entire list. Even though all readers aren't surveyed, a higher response rate from a sample generally produces better and less biased results. This is because you have a better chance of reaching the people who may not read the newsletter. If you do end up surveying all of your readers, be careful when examining the results. If you have a low

In a famous picture, a smiling Harry Truman holds a copy of a freshly printed newspaper reading, "Dewey Defeats Truman." The newspaper wanted to be the first to report the election results. What better way to find out who's going to win than by conducting a survey of voters? Their survey found overwhelming support for Dewey among readers. Their oversight was that very few Truman supporters read their journal. Hence, the survey was biased toward support for Dewey. Well, Dewey never made it to the White House and we have a good example of what can go wrong when you survey the wrong people.

response rate—say between one and 20 percent—your respondents may only be your ardent supporters. There may be a vast difference between your respondents and non-respondents.

Types of Questions

In any survey, you can ask two types of questions: *open ended* or *close ended*. An open ended question lets respondents answer in their own words. It gives them much freedom in answering the question. A close ended question presents respondents with a list of choices, asks them to pick one or more, and leaves space for comments and suggestions. Close ended questions have the advantage of providing answers that are easily summarized. For example, a hospital can survey patients and ask why they chose the facility. The question can be presented as:

Why did you come to this hospital?

[ ] Convenient location

[ ] My doctor recommended it

[ ] You offered a special test or service

[ ] Other _____

The results from this type of question can be easily summarized such as, 32% mentioned "location," 27% mentioned "doctor recommended," 37% mentioned "special service," and 4% listed "other."

Now, if the question was presented in a open ended format, it would appear as:

Why did you choose this hospital? _____

_____

The answers could range from "because my uncle works there," to "reputation." The range of answers, in itself, isn't bad. The difficulty begins when summarizing the survey findings. You'll have to decide whether "reputation" means the same thing as "well-qualified staff" or "you're okay." This is a major disadvantage. But, consider the following situation. A hospital asked an open question for their survey and was surprised to find "good reputation" as the top answer.

> **The ground rules for the use of open versus close ended questions are simple. If you have a large number of questions, make sure that the majority are close ended. Avoid having more than two or three open ended questions. Close ended questions take less time to complete and respondents tire less quickly. Just remember how happy you were in high school or college when you found out the tests would be multiple choice.**

If they had asked the closed question listed previously, they would have led the respondents by the first three options and may not have gotten as strong a response for "reputation."

Check all questions for clarity and wording. The best way to find out is to pretest the questionnaire on four or five people before sending it out. These people don't have to know anything about the subject. A friend or a family member is often the best critic. Pretesting tells you if there are problems with any of the questions and helps you estimate how long it takes to complete the questionnaire. For extensive surveys, consider sending a few photocopied samples before you have the surveys printed. Make changes while they're easy to make.

If you use open ended questions, make sure there is plenty of writing room for your respondents to answer. To give some leeway for your respondents in close ended questions, leave an "other" category at the end, where they can add something. Leave ample room for these responses, too.

Every Question Has a Goal

Make sure every question has a goal and is designed to solicit specific information. For example:

➤ determine true circulation by asking, "Do you regularly pass this newsletter along to someone else?"

➤ measure the effects of word-of-mouth by asking, "Do you regularly discuss items in the newsletter with colleagues or co-workers?"

To develop your newsletter content, ask readers which topics interest them. List possible subjects and ask respondents to check the ones they like. Though your content is strongly influenced by your promotional goals, you can discover article themes through this kind of question.

By having respondents give you information such as title, you can match reader characteristics with the topics they say interest them. This will allow you to reach certain prospects with content that interests them. You may find readers from smaller organizations having different interests than readers from larger ones, engineers having certain concerns that managers don't, and so on.

To determine which topics readers like, provide readers with a list of topics. You can have respondents check which ones they want, rank them in order of interest, or assign a block of points to each.

If you ask readers to check the topics they like, they may check all of them. This gives you little direction. The reader isn't faced with the choice that you as an editor must make—which topics to include and which ones to leave out. One way around this problem is to force the reader to choose, using one of three methods:

1. Give respondents 100 points to distribute among the items. They can give more points to the subjects they prefer. This is the best method in theory, but requires motivated respondents. You also need very precise, lengthy instructions.

2. Tell respondents to choose only a certain number of topics. The problem with this is that you cannot tell exactly which topics were the preferred ones. The respondent only tells you "these five here." You can usually infer general popularity, however, from the number of times a topic is selected.

3. Ask readers to rank topics in order of preference, from "most interesting" to "least interesting." It's fairly easy to rank a small number of topics in order of preference, but gets more difficult as you list more topics.

Some readers may not see that one particular topic in your list they really want. They may just leave the list blank, or be unable to rank them in order. The problem here is not really with the method but with the list itself. Hence, if the list contains ten items, they must be already the "top-ten items." For safety, always include some space where interested readers can add their own topic.

For questions phrased as "how would you rate your interest in…" provide the respondents with a Likert scale. For example, "5" could be "very interesting" and "1" would be "not interesting at all." While researchers disagree on how many categories to provide, they agree that you need to give a full spectrum of replies. For example, it would be wrong to have a 5 point scale, in which "1" was "The newsletter is good" and "5" was "The newsletter is great."

Why Do Your Customers Support You?

It's easy to get caught up in your day-to-day business operations and never give a second thought as to why your customers have chosen you over other alternatives. But, if you're to promote yourself to your existing base, you have to know what you've got that your competitors haven't.

The reason someone *doesn't* buy from you may be just as important to your marketing as why others do. A readership survey can be a very powerful tool for this purpose. Remember, though, that your mailing list may only include people who have supported you in the past. They are likely to purchase, join, donate or vote again. Expand your list of respondents beyond your newsletter list to gather responses to this question.

For example, a computer board manufacturer decided to launch a marketing campaign around its customers' reasons for buying its products. The marketing staff gathered in the conference room to decide why customers bought the products. "Unique features," "technical support," and "ease of use," were mentioned among many. The group finally settled on ease of use. Then, someone in the group suggested surveying customers before the campaign was launched.

The company called 50 of its 1,000 customers. No one mentioned ease of use. In fact, the product was difficult to use. The extra time customers spent installing the product was worth it because they valued the product's reliability. The company's product was far more reliable than any of its competitors'. After studying this feedback, along with statistics on the product's failure rate, the company decided to offer a lifetime guarantee on all of its products. Articles in the newsletter focused on reliability. The guarantee was mentioned in each newsletter.

To find out why people support you, conduct a telephone survey. Call 10 or more of your customers and ask why they chose your services or why they continue to do business with you. This can be done by one person or by dividing the list between several people.

Find out the main benefit that your company offers customers. Ask them specific questions about what you should improve. From prospects, find out why they don't support you. Do they need your type of product or do they buy from a competitor? It is important not to give the impression that this is a sales call. Ultimately, it is. But it the meantime, you must make sure that the person on the other end of the line has the impression you are genuinely interested in why they don't buy from you.

A vintage car parts manufacturer included a survey in its newsletter. The editor asked questions about types of ordering services, shipping, catalogs, brand names, and product categories customers and prospects wanted. He asked why the readers were renovating their automobiles. The survey included questions like, "Are you more interested in maintaining your car's originality or in developing its performance?" The responses helped the company develop its product line and the editor choose the newsletter content.

Many organizations already know their best prospects. Use your prospect list for your survey. You're targeting to precisely the people you want most. Ask them the type of information they need in order to support your organization. Use this information to promote to other donors as well.

For example, a non-profit organization surveyed its top 20 prospective donors to find out what type of information the editor needed to put in the newsletter. Volunteers telephoned prospects with the following question:

"The Shelter provides food, clothing, housing and counseling to children under the age of 18 who would otherwise be on the streets. What type of information would you want before you would consider helping?"

[ ] exactly how donations are appropriated

[ ] more information on the background of the children

[ ] the success rate in counseling and rehabilitating troubled youth

[ ] names of other donors

[ ] more information about our specific needs

[ ] more details on what we provide the children

[ ] other

This information was used to form the best content for generating donations through the newsletter.

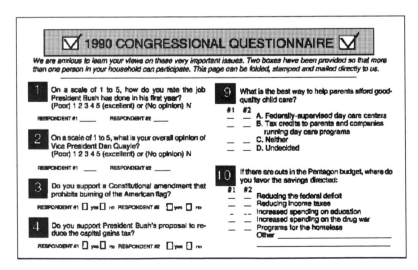

Politicians and lobbying groups are always interested in the opinions of their prospects. The information can be used to help fine-tune campaigns, including the newsletter. Notice how this survey is designed so that two different members of a household can respond.

Feedback from surveys helps you create a newsletter with the overall image you want your customers to have of you. Finding out why prospects don't do business with you can be equally as valuable. They may perceive you as being too small to fulfill their needs, or too big to be responsive. They may not know you provide the services they need. Use your newsletter to overcome these objections. If the respondents find your organization too big, print a story about one of your smaller, satisfied clients.

Determining RISE Levels

Other questions can be used to determine your newsletter's success at each of the RISE promotional levels—Recognition, Image, Specifics and Enactment. Choose questions from the following list to help determine reader's interaction with your newsletter.

R?   Do you read the publication?
[ ] entirely
[ ] almost entirely
[ ] about half
[ ] at least one article
[ ] read passages but seldom complete
[ ] quick scan only
[ ] don't read

R?   How much time do you typically spend reading each issue?
_____ hours. _____ min.

R?   If you don't read the newsletter, why?
[ ] no time
[ ] intend to read it later
[ ] not interested in content
[ ] other _____

I?   How do you usually read the newsletter?

[ ] front to back

[ ] back to front

If a majority of respondents read back to front, place interesting item on the back of each newsletter.

I?   When do you read the newsletter?

[ ] immediately

[ ] read by the end of the day

[ ] read by the end of the weekend

[ ] put in reading stack

[ ] glance through to determine if you'll read it at all

S?   Do you pass along the newsletter to others in your organization?

[ ] yes; to how many? _____

[ ] no

The answers tell you how interesting readers find the newsletter. If it's perceived as helpful, they'll share it with co-workers. If several readers are passing along the publication, add a "route to" box.

S?   Do you discuss content with colleagues?

[ ] yes

[ ] no

S?   How often would you like to receive the newsletter?

[ ] monthly

[ ] every other month

[ ] quarterly

[ ] other _____

S?   Please rate from 1 to 5 your interest in the following features (where 1=not interested and 5=very interested): (*your list*)

S?   Do you save the newsletter?
      [ ] yes
      [ ] no
      [ ] some issues
      This measures how interesting and helpful your newsletter is.

S?   What changes would you like to see?
      [ ] more industry forecasts
      [ ] more product information
      [ ] more photographs
      [ ] cartoons
      [ ] shorter articles
      [ ] leave it as is
      [ ] other _____

E?   In the last year, have you (requested information/attended an
      event/purchased a product or service/volunteered/made a
      donation) as a result of something you read in the newsletter?
      [ ] yes
      [ ] no
      [ ] don't recall

E?   Do you wish to continue receiving the newsletter?
      [ ] yes
      [ ] no
      [ ] only issues specifically covering (subject, product, etc.)
      *Note those that only want specific information. Set up your
      database to code common interests and only mail to these
      readers when you've covered the subjects in your newsletter.*

E?   Would any one else in your organization like to receive this
      newsletter? If so, please add their names and titles below.

Examples of Surveys

Bank Survey. Prior to submitting its yearly marketing budget, a bank used a questionnaire to determine how well its customers were reading its newsletter. The editor knew that the newsletter was generating calls to bank salespeople, but was having trouble getting inquiries tracked. He knew the newsletter budget was going to be under question at a yearly planning meeting and wanted hard data to justify continuing the project. The survey asked how often recipients read the newsletter and how much of it they looked at. It also asked which articles people read and if they passed the newsletter along or discussed its topics with their colleagues.

Because of a tight deadline, the editor didn't have time for a second mailing or follow up procedures. He was mainly concerned with getting questionnaires back that he could show to management. The questionnaire responses justified the bank's expense in continuing production of its newsletter.

Utility Company Survey. An electrical company prints 250,000 newsletters and includes them in monthly bills. After the first year of publishing, the editor wanted to determine if people read the newsletters or if the company should spend its marketing dollars elsewhere. Since cancelling the publication would be a major step, the editor was greatly concerned with statistical accuracy.

The editor contracted with a local marketing service to conduct the survey. The service chose a sample size of 1,000. The survey listed questions asking how much of the newsletter people read, which subjects were interesting, which new subjects they'd like to see. Respondents were given the incentive of a chance to win a stereo. Non-respondents were sent a follow-up questionnaire. Those who still didn't reply were telephoned.

Based on the response to the survey, the editor found that most people were reading the newsletter and received some new suggestions for articles.

Professional Association Survey. A local Chamber of Commerce designed a pre-publication survey to see if members wanted a newsletter. The survey was conducted through a written questionnaire completed as part of the yearly registration process. Members were asked if they wanted only a brief notice of upcoming meetings or a longer publication including business self-help articles. They found that members wanted more than just meeting notices. By asking members which subjects interested them, the Chamber gathered feedback that helped it plan its meeting programs and target prospective members.

In Print or In Person? The Best Method to Conduct Your Survey

The third question asked when designing a formal survey is how are you going to solicit information from readers? Your choices are through mail-back questionnaires, over the phone or in person.

Mail-back Surveys. Mail-back surveys are either included in the newsletter or sent as a separate mailing. Advantages and disadvantages exist for both.

When mailing the survey with the newsletter, you must separate out your sample names from the rest of your list. This can be a hassle, but you need to know which names you sent the questionnaire to for follow-up purposes. It's rare to get a high response after the first mailing.

By sending the survey along with the newsletter, though, readers immediately know what you're inquiring about. They don't have to remember the details of your publication. The response to the survey may also benefit from the goodwill associated with coming in the same bundle as free information. Others argue that readers plan to spend only a certain amount of time reading the newsletter. By including the survey in the same mailing, you either harm your response to the survey or decrease the amount of time the reader spends with the rest of the newsletter.

You can combat this by sending along a sample of an old issue they've already seen. This helps recall the publication without deterring from the time people

The easiest way to conduct a readership survey is to design it to fit on a return post- card. At least once a year, every newsletter publisher should do some type of investi- gating to confirm that the people on the list want the newsletter. Do this by ttaching a postcard to every newsletter. Make it fast and painless to respond.

Please Take 2 Seconds to Answer this Question:

Do you wish to continue receiving this newsletter? ☐ yes ☐ no

Optional 5 seconds more:
How do you think we can improve it:

_____

_____

Please complete or tape business card.

Name:_____

Company: _____

Address:_____

City: _____ State:_____ Zip:_____

spend on the questionnaire. Another option for increasing recognition is to print the survey using the same size, colors and nameplate as your newsletter. You can use the first page for a cover letter about the survey, the two inside pages for the survey and the back of the newsletter for the reader to fold and return the survey to you.

One problem with including the survey along with the newsletter is that those who don't read the newsletter won't see the survey. This is part of the reason why mailed surveys have the lowest response rates of all types of surveys.

If you're in the planning stages, you won't have a newsletter to show respondents. You may be able to find out more information and enjoy a higher response rate by talking to prospective readers in person or over the phone.

Telephone Surveys. To generate a high response rate without much follow-up, conduct your survey by telephone. Phone surveys take less time. Including follow-up, mail surveys can take up to two months to complete. Most phone surveys can be done in a few days.

When talking directly to your prospects, you can either use the same questions as a written survey or you can have more of a general discussion. Regardless of the question format, let your respondent know ahead of time how long the survey will take. Try your best to keep it as short as possible. Most people resent surveys lasting over five minutes. Also remember that respondents are doing you a favor. Make every effort to let them know you appreciate their kindness.

Focus Groups. Focus groups are ideal if you're trying to get a general feel for your readers. These groups can be used if you have local readers or if your readers are already gathered in one location, such as a trade show. By conducting interviews with small groups of people, you can cover more points (legibility, content, layout, story interest, etc.) in greater detail.

Other informal research can be accomplished using one-on-one interviews, or interviews with a few consumers or supporters simultaneously. Ask staff members for feedback during day-to-day conversations. Have your representatives ask about the newsletter as part of taking an order, enlisting a new member, or receiving a donation. Or you can randomly conduct spot checks by telephoning readers. Informal research can be as easy as mingling at a trade show, in a shopping mall or answering the phone for a few days and talking to readers.

Increasing Your Response Rate

Surveys often suffer from low response rates. This in itself is not necessarily bad. For example, if you have contacted 100,000 individuals and gotten a 3% response rate, you still have a sample of 300 people. However, if you only have a list of 100 names, and you have the same 3% response rate, you only have three people to work with.

Here are three ways to increase your response rate:

> keep the survey short and non-intrusive
> provide incentives to reply
> conduct a follow-up

The written questionnaire should look professional. This tells respondents that the results are important. It should be typeset to minimize the physical impression of length and to increase the ease and speed of completion. Keep the length to one page. State within the instructions how long it will take to complete the survey.

Begin the questionnaire with easy questions such as title and company information. Write as many of the questions with closed answers and give the reader boxes to check. This encourages the respondents to continue when they see how quickly they're moving through the questionnaire. Save the open questions, such as "why are you a member of the professional association?" for the end.

Being polite is the best way to be non-intrusive. Over the phone, it's simply a matter of acknowledging that your respondent may be busy with something else. For example your telephone introduction could go something like this, "Hello, Ted. My name is Sandra Smith with Advanced Computer Associates. I want to ask you how we can improve the services you require. I have a few questions to ask you and wonder if you have three minutes to talk?"

Return Survey & Receive a Free Clip-on Flashlight!

Please complete survey on reverse side, fold, tape, and mail. For your convenience, postage has been pre-paid.

Your suggestions will be used to update future issues of this newsletter. Thank you for your input.

Incentives also increase response rate. When each respondent wins something, the response will usually be higher than with promised incentives such as prize drawings. Drawings are only effective if the prize is substantial and respondents feel they have a good chance of winning. In one survey, for example, the incentive was a drawing of a product worth $500. In a second example, each person who returned the survey received a mini-flashlight worth about $1. The first survey had a initial response rate of 3% while the second enjoyed a 14% response.

An incentive commonly used is a crisp $1 bill attached to the survey. This approach should double your response and result in a rate between 35% and 50%. The dollar bill works best since you pre-mail the incentive to everyone versus only mailing to respondents who list their name.

Along with using incentives, follow-up techniques can help your response rate. About 10 days after the initial mailing, mail all non-respondents a reminder card that emphasizes the importance of the study and of a high response rate.

An event planning consultant sent out a survey that qualified prospects and asked what they wanted to read in the newsletter. A free booklet, "51 Proven Tips for a Successful Company Event" was offered as an incentive to complete the survey.

If confidentiality is not important to your customers, keep track of those who have replied to the survey and send a second copy of the survey to non-respondents. You can number each questionnaire and only mail again to those whose questionnaires are not returned within three weeks. Usually, between 75% and 85% of the eventual return should be back by this time. From this, you can predict the final response rate from the first mailing.

When confidentiality is important, send the second mailing to the entire sample with a note to respondents to ignore this request if they've already returned the initial survey.

A better method of tracking responses, while assuring confidentiality, is by using postcards along with your survey. Send readers a standard questionnaire without a number. Attach to the questionnaire a numbered postcard. Instruct the respondent to complete the questionnaire and separately mail both the questionnaire and the postcard on the same day. The postcard could read:

> "Dear Researcher: I am sending this postcard at the same time I am putting my completed questionnaire in the mail. Since my questionnaire is completely anonymous, this postcard will tell you that I am one of the people who have responded to your survey. "

This procedure maintains the respondent's anonymity. At the same time, it tells you when someone has completed the questionnaire.

If you still have a response rate below 75%, the next step is to call the remaining non-respondents and conduct the survey over the telephone.

Using Results for Improved Promotions

For most editors, there's a great excitement in getting feedback from readers. Many editors are isolated on a day-to-day basis from readers. Returned surveys are a welcome change. But often, by the time all of the answers are in, many editors are tired of the survey and never implement the new suggestions. This is especially true if the replies showed nothing drastic to change.

What will you do with your results? They often serve as a way to understand your readers better. If you get an overwhelmingly negative response, it's time to go back through the planning stages. Re-evaluate your project, including your need for a newsletter.

Most results are supportive. With carefully scrutiny, though, you can find some good ideas to put to use.

If your survey is an extensive data collection effort, you may want to involve a research firm or local college. Either one can computerize the data and generate statistically accurate results. Most surveys can be analyzed by simply noting the number of people who answered each question a certain way. Say you sampled 210 people and received a 100% response. The results show 150 people skim the newsletter,

The owner of a Japanese restaurant surveyed customers to find out why they came to the restaurant. He found that they were strongly influenced by the children's love for the "show" the chefs put on. In this survey, he found out two important facts: families were a good target market and his newsletter should emphasize the theatrical abilities of his restaurant's chefs.

50 read it cover to cover, and 10 never read it. You can say with reasonable confidence that 71% of all readers skim the newsletter, 24% read it entirely, and 5% never read it.

You may want to analyze more than one question at a time. In a survey prepared by an event planner, respondents were asked the number of special events they held each year. They were also asked to check their type of business. This information was combined using a cross-tabulation chart to see which types of businesses held the most special events. The event planner used the data to target her most active prospects.

Present the results of your survey as quickly as possible. Include a note in the next newsletter issue thanking those who responded. In addition, respond directly to the suggestions. Promptness enhances your image as a responsive organization.

Regardless of the type of scouting you use, you're going to learn about your readers. Although it's often frightening at first, leaving the shelter of your office and reaching out to discover more about your readers is an enlightening experience. Readers give you ideas you would never think up on your own. Knowing them better makes producing a newsletter more fun. It also gives you confidence to pick up the phone and interview other people for your newsletter articles.

With this knowledge and confidence in hand, you will produce a newsletter that brings in revenues for your organization.

7

Mailing Lists: Choosing the Best Mountain Climbers

The promotional power of your newsletter is only as strong as your mailing list. You need qualified, able-bodied climbers on your mountain. Climbers who are along for the interesting sights, but who have no interest or influence in taking final action, won't help you achieve your goals. To achieve maximum potential, take great pains to find qualified names for your list. That said, you must also regularly update the list.

Creating Your "House" List

Your house list is the one you compile yourself. It includes names of many of the people already on your mountain—customers, prospects, suppliers and other people who can influence your sales.

Customers & Prospects. The most important names to get on your list are your prospects and clients or supporters. If more than one person influences the decision to support your organization or purchase your services, don't limit your list to just one contact per company. Find each person who influences the decision. Because your client base is a dynamic entity, your mailing list should be reviewed frequently, adding new clients, members and prospects, while deleting invalid names.

When adding to the list, make sure all have complete names, addresses and zip codes. Some larger organizations require mail stops or the piece will be considered undeliverable and

> **"As direct marketing professionals like to joke, the three most important facets of direct-mail campaigns are lists, lists and lists."—Allen Miller**

One publisher was dumbfounded when his newsletter didn't generate any response in spite of several aggressive marketing techniques. After further questioning, he admitted that his mailing list consisted only of company names and addresses; no individual names were on the list. He assumed the company owners would automatically get the newsletters, even without the name!

thrown away. Also keep track of personnel changes such as new titles and names. Using the correct name and title will please your prospects. With telephone rates decreasing and mailing rates on the rise, it is cheaper to screen an address than to mail a "dead" piece for an entire year.

Remember to put only those prospects on the list whom you would want as customers or members. Along with other characteristics, determine the geographical area of your sales territory and mail only within this area.

In addition to your clients and prospects, you should send your newsletter to several other strategic places.

Suppliers. Keep suppliers informed of your progress. Send your newsletter to your accountants, attorneys, bankers and other subcontractors. They may be able to provide you with suggestions on your new products and services. In addition, your suppliers' salespeople are one of your best sources for referrals.

Remember to include the vendors who help you with the newsletter. Tell your printer and mailing service you've added them to the list, asking them to evaluate the newsletter's condition when it arrives. They may spot problems with equipment or suggest changes that improve the newsletter's chances of making it through the mail in good condition. Putting the mail house on the list may make them more quality conscious concerning folding or labeling.

Employees. Make sure your newsletter is always distributed to employees, especially salespeople, prior to mailing. This avoids the embarrassment of a prospect inquiring about an item in the newsletter and the staff being unfamiliar with the topic. Stress to employees the importance of reading and understanding the articles in the newsletter.

If reasonable, send the newsletter to your employees' homes rather than handing them out at work. This helps the families know more about your organization.

Be sure to add your own name to the list so you know when the newsletter is delivered and in what condition. If you mail your newsletter nationwide, add a friend across the country to see how long it takes to make the trip.

The Press. By sending your newsletter to the press, editors and reporters will know of your company and may remember it when writing special industry articles. Even if you have a small local market, having your company mentioned by local media helps relationships with bankers and makes it easier to recruit top people.

Have a separate list to mail to influential people in your industry such as trade journal editors, newsletter writers, and local radio, TV and newspaper editors. When sending to large newspapers or magazines, make sure you research the name and address of a specific editor who reviews material in your field. If you're mailing your newsletter bulk rate, mail these newsletters first class. The media rely on and appreciate timely news.

When you send the first issue of your newsletter to the press, include a personalized cover letter providing a background statement on your organization and telling why the individual has been added to your list. Leave a space at the bottom of the letter for recipients to add other names from their organizations to your list.

Non-competing Organizations. Non-competing, complementary organizations are those who do well when you do well. Keeping these people informed is good for your business. In the healthcare field, for instance, many doctors recommend other specialists. These two medical practices are complementary. Most organizations have complementary partners. For some fields, these are less obvious and require more ingenuity to find.

Ask vendors of complementary products if they want to trade lists or offer to do a co-mailing. To entice others to give you their mailing list, create a special issue of your newsletter focusing on their organization and products describing how they work with yours.

Community. Mail your newsletter to community leaders such as political representatives, professional associations and market research firms.

Send a copy to every library in your area on a regular basis. You may be surprised how many people will read it. Follow up to make sure it's being set out on the shelves.

> A manufacturer sent a cover letter along with its newsletter to a list of 50 editors. The letter included a reply card where other names could be added. Several of the publications responded with additional names and comments. One magazine called to request permission to reprint one of the newsletter articles. Thousands of dollars worth of publicity came from spending a few dollars a year to send one carefully targeted newsletter.

Get Other People to Send it for You. Some companies are reluctant to release lists of their salespeople, dealers and distributors. They may agree, however, to mail your newsletter to these lists for you. Many organizations have been able to increase their distribution using this approach.

If you offer a service to businesses, consider sending multiple copies to consultants or others who may distribute them to their clients. One publisher sent several copies of an advertising agency newsletter to a management consultant. The consultant showed it to the clients he was working with. The agency acquired two stable, $25,000/year clients by printing an extra 15 newsletters.

The first time you work with another organization or a consultant, send along a cover letter thanking them for their help with distribution.

Free Lists. If you're a member of a trade association or Chamber of Commerce, you may be able to get the membership list free or you may already have it in a directory.

If free lists aren't available, you may choose to expand your distribution by renting a valuable mailing list.

Finding a Targeted Mailing List

In addition to your own list, you can find the climbers of other people's mountains. You can rent the mailing lists of trade associations, industry journals, business directories, other organizations. Find an association or journal that caters to your targeted readers. Call the organization and ask if they rent their mailing lists. Some will refer you to a mailing list broker who handles the rental for them. When you talk with the broker, find out if they have similar lists of your prospects from different sources.

Look for organizations promoting their services to the same prospects as you. Call them and ask if you can rent their mailing list. Some organizations, such as medical practices, must keep their list confidential. If you operate a medical practice, look at other ways to find new patients. People moving into a new area are good prospects. Look in the Yellow Pages under "mailing lists" to find a broker who handles the names of new residents. These names are available free from utility companies in some areas.

Charities have the challenge of keeping mailings small and targeted. Mailing to every resident of a certain area is too expensive. Look at other organizations who have donors with similar interests. Members of an animal rights organization may also be interested in preserving the environment for animals as well as people. Call other charities and see if they'll sell their list or exchange it for yours.

Look in the *Book of Directories* available at most libraries. See if any of the available directories match your targeted audience.

Mailing lists of periodicals usually have the most current and accurate names and addresses since it's to the recipient's advantage to provide it. Many periodicals have additional information on their readers. This allows you to create a more targeted list. Ask them to sort on size of company, products they use or sell, titles, or whatever other categories they collect. If you know the characteristics of your best prospects—such as title, geographic location, company size—rent only the names that meet your criteria.

The sales representatives of some publications will want you to advertise in their journal in order to rent the list. Don't reject this idea immediately. You can use the advertisement to reinforce the promotions in your newsletter.

If you rent a mailing list for your newsletter, remember that the recipients are not as familiar with your organization as your customers, members and other prospects. To help avoid confusion and increase the effectiveness of the mailing, include a cover letter along with the first issue you send. Use it to introduce your organization and its products and services. This will save room in the newsletter and will avoid boring the readers who are already familiar with you. One company learned this first hand when conducting a reader's survey. They had rented a list from a magazine and had been mailing to the names for almost a year when they conducted the survey. Many of those surveyed said they were unsure of what products the company produced, even though a product list appeared in each issue.

In addition to those from magazines, consumer and business lists are available. Consumer lists are compiled from such sources as census surveys, zip codes and automobile registrations. Business lists consist of names taken from the Yellow Pages, business and trade directories, trade show registrations and association rosters. A good source for both is through list brokers.

List brokers keep abreast of the list marketplace and have information about how and where to buy the best lists for your needs. Some brokers even specialize in markets such as computers, medical or legal. The best way to locate a good broker is by referral. They can also be found in the Yellow Pages under "mailing lists" and in a directory published by the Standard Rate and Data Service called *Direct Mail List Rates and Data*.

When renting through a broker, find out when the list was last updated. Sometimes, list owners and brokers will guarantee that a certain percentage be deliverable. For some markets you can find response lists. These lists contain names of people who have made purchases by mail. Response lists typically have a higher response rate than other rented lists because the people have already responded to direct mail. Response lists are also typically more expensive than compiled or subscription lists.

The cost of renting mailing lists varies greatly depending on the source, type and size of the list you wish to rent. Costs are usually determined on a per-thousand name basis and can be as low as $20 or as high as $180 per 1,000 names for one time use. Mailing lists on disk are usually cheaper than lists printed on labels. If you want to mail several issues to the same list, you can usually negotiate a lower price when renting several copies of the list at the same time. However, you won't have the benefit of receiving updates.

With a bit of digging, you can find good mailing lists to rent. Having more well-qualified climbers on your mountain is more than worth the additional cost.

Free Ways to Reach More Prospects

Become aware of all potential climbers. Discover ways to reach them without renting mailing lists. Beyond mailing, you can extend the penetration of your newsletter in several ways.

Encourage Sharing. Exposure is often increased by people saving or passing along your publication to others. Adding a "route to" box is one possible way to encourage sharing within an organization. You can also provide a coupon for those receiving the pass-along copies. They can use it to add their name to your list.

In this Issue:	Route to:
Clearing Canada Customs	_____
Preparing Int'l. Shipments	_____
Document Shipping Tips	_____
UPS Drop-Off Boxes	_____
C.O.D. Service	_____

United Parcel Service puts a "route to" box next to the listing of articles. The box makes it easy for readers to pass along the newsletter to others. By putting the "route to" information in the same box as the contents, recipients can even note specific articles the other readers should look at.

Piggyback. To save postage and increase exposure, you can enclose your newsletter with another promotional mailing or with monthly statements or invoices. You probably receive several newsletters this way from utility companies, investment firms and credit card issuers.

Press Release. You can attract new subscribers by sending news releases about your newsletter to publications in your field. Some magazines will list it in their literature section. Using this approach, you must have a mechanism to assure that responses are qualified and won't be a waste of postage and printing.

Hand Outs. Newsletters can be handed out at trade shows and conventions or offered to seminar producers to include as giveaways. They can be used as leave-behinds by salespeople. Always have people from your company hand out copies when speaking at seminars, meetings and conventions. Keep a stack of newsletters in your lobby for new vendors, prospective employees and walk-in clients.

Unexpected Requests. Always print and save extra copies of each of your publications. Put them in a secure place so that if someone needs a particular issue, a copy is available for photocopying. This serves as a good reference of subjects already covered. You may even find them a good training source for new employees.

Reply Cards. When renting a mailing list, using other people's lists, handing out newsletters to groups, or leaving stacks of newsletters for browsers, remember to include a sign-up card so you can add interested readers to your list. Make sure the readers know they have to return the card to get onto the list. Legally, the names of people who respond belong to you.

A distributor uses a reply card for readers to request their catalog. The names sent in are checked against those on the newsletter list. Those not on the list are added.

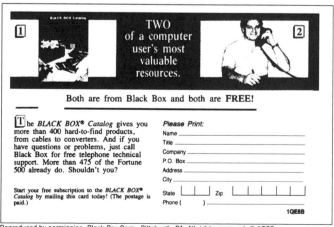

Saving Money by Pruning Your List

The best way to avoid frequent pruning of your mailing list is to add only qualified names to begin with. Once that's done, periodically check to see if your prospect is still at the same address and make sure they're still a valid prospect.

Every now and then, you'll need to send a climber home. The reply cards used in building a list are also helpful in pruning one. Up to 25% of the names or addresses on your list will become outdated each year. If you are going to publish an on-going newsletter, you will have to update and prune your list at least once a year, preferably more often.

Higher postage costs are increasing the need for accurate lists. By ensuring that every newsletter reaches a targeted reader, you make efficient use of your postage dollars.

You may want to use a reply card to validate address information and re-qualify your recipients. A form like this can help you keep your list updated.
Those who don't respond by mail can be sent a postcard and asked to call to remain on the list.

ATTENTION READER

*I*n order to receive future issues of *Multiuser PC News*, the publication for Arnet standard multiuser computing, please fill out the following qualification form. All questions must be answered in order to be eligible for this FREE one year subscription.

*T*he *Multiuser PC News* is the only publication dealing exclusively with the multiuser PC market. Published bi-monthly, the *MUPCN* supplies you with first hand information on new hardware and software products; sales, marketing, and distribution information; dealer profiles and editorial opinion.

All questions must be answered to qualify for a FREE one year subscription ($32 value). Please return immediately.

Name_____
Signature_____ Date_____
Title_____
Company_____
Address_____
City_____
State_____ Zip_____
Phone (___)_____

The most effective tools I use to generate sales are:
- ☐ Media Advertising (Magazines, Radio, TV)
- ☐ Direct Mail Advertising (Brochures, Flyers, etc.)
- ☐ Directories, Buyer's Guides
- ☐ Company Newsletter
- ☐ Trade Shows
- ☐ Seminars
- ☐ Direct Sales
- ☐ Telemarketing
- ☐ Word of Mouth/Referral
- ☐ Other_____

I am a:
- ☐ End user
- ☐ Dealer
- ☐ Distributor
- ☐ Value-added reseller
- ☐ Software OEM
- ☐ Hardware OEM
- ☐ Consultant
- ☐ MIS Manager
- ☐ Owner/Employee of Computer Retail Store
- ☐ Other_____

Number of employees at my location:
- ☐ 1-9
- ☐ 10-19
- ☐ 20-49
- ☐ 50-99
- ☐ 100-999
- ☐ 1000 or more

Number of years in business:
- ☐ 1-4 years
- ☐ 5-9 years
- ☐ 10-19 years
- ☐ 20 years or more

The publication(s) I read most frequently are:
- ☐ InfoWorld
- ☐ BYTE
- ☐ PC Week
- ☐ PC World
- ☐ MIS Week
- ☐ Unix Review
- ☐ Unix World
- ☐ Micro Marketworld
- ☐ Computer Retail News
- ☐ Computer+Software News
- ☐ Computer Decisions
- ☐ Computer World
- ☐ PC Tech Journal
- ☐ Others_____

My primary job function is:_____

Within the next 12 months, I plan to use/resell a multiuser operating system for the IBM PC or compatible:
- ☐ Yes ☐ No

If yes, the multiuser operating system of my choice is:
- ☐ Unix
- ☐ Xenix
- ☐ MBOS-5
- ☐ Pick
- ☐ Theos (Oasis)
- ☐ Venix/86
- ☐ MUC-DOS
- ☐ Coherent
- ☐ QNX
- ☐ Mumps
- ☐ Other_____

Some direct marketers never remove a name from their mailing list except by specific request or when the piece is returned as undeliverable. Their statistics show that as long as a mailing is reaching someone, it may be read and produce results often enough to justify keeping all inactive names on a list. Obviously, this can work for mass appeal items like clothing and food, but most newsletters are written for highly targeted audiences. For example, the new occupant of Joe's Meat Store may be a vegetarian restaurant and won't care about your *Beefeaters' News.*

Aside from using reply cards and qualification forms, another way to keep a bulk mailing list clean is to add "Address Correction Requested" or "Return Postage Guaranteed" under your return address. Contact the post office to find the fees involved and the specific format to use. Without the address correction notice, the post office will discard the bulk mail piece and you'll never know it's not being delivered.

Up to this point, we've looked at your organization's goals and abilities to produce a newsletter. We've also examined the characteristics of your best readers and different ways to reach them. The next step is to combine this information to determine the best content for your newsletter.

8

Balancing Promotional Content With News

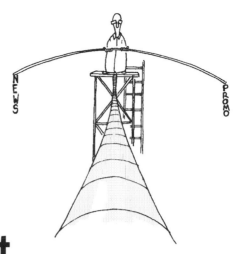

With all you've established—your promotional goals, capabilities, prospects, reader interests, etc.—you can map out effective content for your ideal promotional publication.

It's easy to fall into the trap of scrambling to write your newsletter just to get it in the mail. Don't lose sight of your road map. Take the time to choose the content of your newsletter carefully. It's critical to promoting through image and specific techniques.

Proclaim Your Purpose With a Name & Subtitle

Once you've chosen a subject, clearly tell your readers what it is. Include this in the nameplate. Your newsletter's name should tell readers what kind of information it contains, to whom it's addressed, and what your product, service or purpose is.

Some titles are very creative while others are more simple. Both get the job done. For example, the name of a newsletter for a plastics manufacturer can be as simple as *Plastic Product News*, with a line below "For buyers of molded plastic products." It can also be as creative as *Out of the Mold*, with the same subtitle.

The following are several examples of newsletter names along with their subtitles. Some are straightforward, others are more clever. Notice how the subtitles clarify the name of

Here's the key to content: from the choice of interesting routes to take, fill your newsletter with only those leading to your final destination—your promotional goals.

the publication. Think about how long it would take a new reader to figure out the scope of the publication without it. Notice how some of the subtitles promote with words like "exclusive" and "opportunities."

➤ *News Splash*
Tips for painless pool and spa maintenance for homeowners
Pools & Spas Unlimited

➤ *House & Home*
Ideas for better living for Citibank Classic cardmembers
Citibank

➤ *Managing Growth*
Management ideas & techniques to help companies grow
Ernst & Associates

➤ *The Franklin Investor*
Insights & opportunities for investors of the Franklin Group of Funds
The Franklin Group of Funds

➤ *FUNDamentals*
An exclusive publication for Kemper Shareholders
Kemper Family of Funds

➤ *Direct Success*
Quarterly tips & techniques for profitable direct mail marketing
Lakewood Lists

➤ *RoundUPS*
Published quarterly for customers & friends of United Parcel Service
United Parcel Service

➤ *The Rolling Phone*
News for cellular phone users from Cellular One
Cellular One

➤ *MGB Newsletter*
Published for MGB enthusiasts by The Roadster Factory
The Roadster Factory

Some newsletters have a word in the title that instantly tells the reader that the contents of the publication are newsworthy. Most of the following list was borrowed from newspaper names and feature headlines. Consider them when naming your publication.

Advocate, Announcer, Briefing, Broadcast, Bulletin, Comment, Communicator, Communique, Courier, Clip, Dateline, Dispatch, Examiner, Facts, Flash, Focus, Forum, Highlights, Hotline, In Brief, Inside, Keynotes, Letter, Line, Link, Message, Messenger, Monthly, News, Newsbrief, Newsline, Notes, Observer, Perspective, Profile, Relay, Release, Report, Reporter, Review, Scene, Scope, Spotlight, Talk, Transmit, Update, View, Vision, Voice, Wire, Word

In addition to news titles, look for words that tell the reader a benefit to reading. Powerful marketing words for business newsletters are:

Profit, Money, Growth, Success, Wealth, Thrive, Save, Free, Results, Easy, Fast

Words that help promote to volunteers and donors are:

Improve, Change, Influence, Impact, Make a Difference, Breakthroughs, Forward, Inspire, Brighten, Make a Mark, Affect

Keep these words in mind for titles, features and articles as well as for your title and subtitle.

Not all newsletters effectively identify their intentions. For example, I picked up a newsletter about Power Bars in a bicycle shop once and couldn't figure out what a "Power Bar" was. Because the newsletter was in a cycling store, I first assumed they were talking about customized handle bars. Then I saw an article in the publication about how Billy Idol used them for training and assumed it was a weight lifting system. I scanned the nameplate and the masthead, I looked for a small ad, anything, but I couldn't find a clue. Then, buried in one of the articles, the writer talked about *eating* them! Ah-ha. Candy bars. This must have taken 15 minutes.

The publisher could have avoided my search by adding the subtitle to *Power Bar News*, "How athletes can achieve maximum performance with Power Bar high-energy snacks."

Seeking Help

Because the name of your newsletter is something you probably won't change, ask for feedback from several people. Take the time to create a name that you really like. Some organizations seek the help of an advertising or public relations agency. Others have internal naming contests.

If you have a contest, be sure to set some guidelines concerning the marketing message. You want it to include the specialty covered by the newsletter and the audience type. Offer a prize for the best name, but clearly state that the name may or may not be used for the newsletter. This way, if you aren't satisfied with any of the names submitted in the contest, you won't feel pressured to use them. At the very least, contest results provide ideas that can lead to a variation you like.

The Meat of Your Newsletter

The name of your newsletter is important because your readers notice it first. Start your communication process here and lead readers to the image level where they skim the content. Like hikers going through the sacked lunches you've given them, once you've attracted your readers interest, they open up the sandwich and peer inside. Peanut butter and jelly? Roast beef? Pastrami?

To choose the filling for your newsletter, apply the knowledge you collected about your readers. The publisher of a pharmaceutical publication, for example, found that physicians already stay abreast of changes in medicine. Instead of including general medical news, the newsletter exclusively covers the applications of their new drugs.

If your goal is to promote a variety of products to several markets, you may rotate the products you feature from issue to issue. You could also have different sections for each market. By segmenting topics within your newsletter, readers get used to finding the articles of interest to them. From a promotional standpoint, each section tells targeted readers how you can solve their unique problems.

If the characteristics of your readers aren't easily summarized, try other techniques to attract as many readers as possible. Some publishers rank news items by the greatest amount of overall interest. The most popular articles go on the front page, the middle group go inside, and the remainder are condensed into news bulletins.

Many organizations have the challenge of balancing technical and nontechnical articles to reach a wider range of readership. Associations have to serve both seasoned professionals and newcomers. Many industrial and high tech companies sell to technical audiences as well as to those in administration or management. Let your audience mix tell you how to balance the information for both types.

Learn to put aside your own interests. Often writers feel a need to jazz up or humanize a technical article. Differentiate whether a subject is truly dull to your audience or just dull to you. If you attempt to make a review of a new laser welder read like a feature from *Life*, your engineer readers may question your expertise. On the other hand, if you're trying to tell potential donors about the plights of the homeless, show the people's discomfort to generate donations. Show the urgency for donor's help by appealing to their emotions.

Find the information that works and present it in a way that attracts your readers' attention. Pack articles full of promotional punch, from the writing style to the visuals you choose. This is the challenge of newsletter editing.

Weaving Promotional Information With News

Promotional newsletters walk a fine line between soft-sell and unbiased information. While you want the unique features of your products and services to appear in as many articles as possible, it's the useful information that keeps your readers coming back for more.

Walking the fine line between marketing and news copy is tricky. When you go too far to the promotional side, you end up with what readers consider a brochure or company propaganda. When you go too far to the "news" side, you're wasting your marketing dollars. Don't confuse your publication with industry tabloids and magazines.

Newsletters are also not the same as popular magazines. Readers don't expect newsletters to be helpful in passing idle time. One of my clients once asked if her newsletter should include a recipe. "Sure," I said, "…as long as you sell groceries or offer consulting on nutrition."

In other words, keep in mind the difference between your promotional newsletter and a subscription newsletter. If people are paying for a publication, they expect it to be packed with useful information. While you want to include helpful information in your newsletter, always make sure it has at least some tie back to your product, organization or industry.

Promoting Within Specific Topics

Your newsletter's subject is the link back to your organization. When all content follows the main subject, readers feel a clear sense of purpose. It also eases the job of selecting specific topics.

Newsletter content can be broken down into six main categories:

> ➤ product (including services, causes or ideas)
> ➤ customer
> ➤ support
> ➤ organization & people
> ➤ industry
> ➤ reader service

Draw topics for your articles from these areas.

Within each article, squeeze in the reasons readers should buy from you. Adapt them to attract prospects, too. There are basic assurances you need to give prospects. They want to know that your product or service solves their needs and that you can deliver what you're promoting. Many prospects need to know that you won't abandon them after they buy, donate, vote or join. Perhaps having a convenient location is important to them.

Remember that you have limited time to capture readers. If your main points can be handled more quickly by a table or graph, design one and use the caption to say what little still needs words. For example, a phone company showed readers the cost of its various calling plans in a table format. The editor promoted all of the company's services while also helping readers save money.

To win additional business from current customers, provide different assurances. Persuade customers that it's not a risk to give one supplier all of their business. Ensure customers you can offer more than one area of expertise. If you can save them time and money by providing more than one service or product, this may weigh in your favor. Also, the fact that the customer already knows you makes buying from you less of a risk.

To maintain the same level of business from existing clients you must provide them with other decisive information. Restate that you appreciate their business. Convince them that your growth brings them increased, not decreased, service. Give them insight into your future plans and show how you're keeping their needs in mind when making changes. Ask customers, voters, members, and donors how you can serve their needs better.

Depending on the goals of your publication, include this type of assurance in the various types of articles. In addition to the assurances, also keep in mind your target promotional level. Each of the six types of articles should operate within the four levels of marketing:

➣R   Recognition: who you are

➣I   Image: what you provide

➣S   Specifics: how your service works

➣E   Enactment: what action to take

If one of your goals is to talk about the capabilities and virtues of your organization, the best way to demonstrate them is through your products and services. Within product and service articles, you can discuss the talents that went into designing them. On the other hand, if you talk only about your capabilities without backing them up with concrete examples, the result is a "hot air" publication. Readers usually let these braggy newsletters just blow on by. To keep reader interest, use product articles that *show* rather than *tell* about your organization.

Touting Your Products, Services, Events, Causes & Ideas

"Specifics" fall under the category of articles on products, services, ideas and causes. The articles of manufacturers, professional services and healthcare providers cover new additions or changes to existing products, services or equipment. For non-profit organizations, your articles will feature the services you provide to your members or community. Associations usually offer specifics on events such as meetings or seminars.

In every article, tell readers your name and the name of your product, service or cause. Give readers specific information. Show how a product works. Interview people helped by donors. At some point in the story, tell prospects how to request more information, give you their support or make a purchase.

Explain your products and services either with words or with visuals. Putting information into a table or graph, instead of writing it up, presents it more quickly to readers.

Products. Articles on products can either be on new products or updates to existing ones. When structuring an article, remember the RISE promotional levels. Within the text, repeat the name of your company and the name of your product line. Tell why the product is unique and what specific need it solves. Share your reasoning for developing the product. Tell how it came from the ideas and requests from customers. List potential applications or users. If one is available, show a photograph of the product in use. All potential users will be interested in product details. Explain how to order or call for more details.

Before the days of its four-color magazine, Aldus used its newsletter, *The Desktop Publisher*, to announce new versions of PageMaker. The company listed ordering information in a column running alongside the write-up the new product. The main article continued inside and detailed more features. Since software is difficult to show, a photograph of the product's box was shown on the front page. Diagrams were used on the continuing page.

Since product articles are important to increase awareness and boost sales, be creative in showing your products in as many issues of your newsletter as possible. Search for new angles to talk about the features of the same product.

How the Weatherloy Family of Resins Help Outdoor Furniture

The Weatherloy family of resins are designed for outdoor use by Washington Penn Plastic. The plastic compound is used by manufacturers for customers who want durable, reliable outdoor furniture that keeps its appearance and is easy to clean. Here's what goes in it and why.

Mineral Fillers:
Either talc, calcium carbonate, or a combination of both are used to give the furniture rigidity.

Polypropylene:
Both homopolymer and copolymer grades are used either together or separately to provide the furniture with impact resistance and "toughness."

UV Stabilizers:
UV additives improve polypropylene's resistance to sunlight, extending furniture's useful life.

Antistats:
Antistat additives make the furntiure easier to keep clean by lessening polypropylene's tendency to collect dust.

For more information, contact your sales representative or call Washington Penn Plastic at (412) 228-1260.

The weathering properties of Weatherloy are tested by devices such as South Florida Test Service's Sun[R]. Ten focused mirrors concentrate natural sunlight onto samples mounted in the target area. The machine tracks the sun to maximize the sample's exposure to radiant energy. The Sun[R] accelerates weathering from three to 13 times.

Speaking of South Florida Test Services, Washington Penn's own research scientist Dave Warfel spoke at a seminar sponsored by the service. He spoke to chemists from major chemical companies about Washington Penn's efforts in designing resilient plastics for outdoor furniture and automotive parts.

South Florida Test Services can be reached at (305) 824-3900.

Some manufacturers devote entire articles to possible applications of parts or materials. Others include background articles on how the materials work. Sometimes this includes a history of the technology. One manufacturer listed the main "ingredients" in one of its plastic formulations. The plastic was designed to withstand outdoor conditions. Following each technical name, the benefits of the additive were listed in non-technical terms. The explanation included a photograph and an explanation of the equipment used to test exposure to sunlight.

Along with your current offerings, your existing customers need to know what new products you're working on. By providing readers with advanced information, your newsletter will be valued more by prospects. Selling additional products or services can be as easy as providing your prospects with this crucial information. Later, when the new invention is ready to ship, you can officially announce it in the newsletter.

Services. Service articles are structured similarly to product stories. Their purpose is to restate and explain the services you provide. For existing customers, service articles give an idea of all of the things you do. A customer using your bookkeeping and tax services, for example, may not know that you also offer investment advice.

From a marketing perspective, it's important that your services have names. Names help clarify that your service is a "product." A business consultant, for example can offer the "5-Week Turnaround Program" for struggling companies. "Hit the Ground Running" is for start-up ventures. For improved corporate communications, the expert can package the "Through the Grapevine Program." Notice how the names give you a better feel for the consultant's services. They explain and promote better than saying, "We provide consultation services to businesses of all sizes."

Along with the name of the service, tell who the service is for and what benefits they'll receive by using it. If you have competition, explain how your service is unique. Because some of your articles may be previews, specify when each service is available and how to buy or get more information.

For most organizations, your services are your products. Hospitals promote new tests and procedures. Banks explain various types of loans. Financial planners discuss investment opportunities. Associations offer advice and support.

Causes. Politicians, churches and other community groups write articles on the causes they advocate. It's often difficult to get people to take action for the benefit of one's community or the world. People usually respond best when the benefit is for themselves. Sometimes, to inspire the community activist latent in everyone, you have to take drastic steps. Other times, it's just a matter of educating people about a problem.

A local politician promoted his administration by listing all of the legislation he had proposed. Most voters have to wait for election time to find out what their representative has done during the term. A regular update can pave the way for a politician's reelection campaign.

Articles on ideas and causes try to sway public opinion. You ask readers to change the way they vote or increase the money they contribute. Articles are structured to tell what you believe in, how your organization is making improvements, and why reader's support is urgent. Timely articles are a must. Readers must take action immediately in order for you to maximize support.

Promote by Showing Your Supporters

The most effective way to promote your products, services or causes is by showing examples of the people or causes you've helped. Much of the same information found in specifics articles can be given through the testimonials of your supporters. Show your clients or supporters through case histories, profiles, customer news and by welcoming new customers or members.

Case Histories. Case histories are your success stories. They explain how a client saved money, solved problems or increased sales by using your product or services. The person or company in your case history essentially does the promoting for you.

A case history covers the problem your client had and how you helped solve it. At the end of the article, let your readers know three things: you solved the problem discussed; you can easily be contacted to begin solving similar problems; and any other benefits to working with you.

It's important to choose your case histories carefully. Either select rare applications which challenge the limits of your product or common applications applying to most of your readers. Rare occurrences are usually intriguing. Common applications attract readers with similar problems. To feature a common application, take your readers' most common need and find a satisfied customer who is willing to be featured.

> The newsletter of a charity combined the case histories of two families to explain the problems of hunger in Bolivia. The articles told about the plights of the families and how donations had helped.

Donations to community groups increase when they highlight the individuals they are helping. People relate to pictures and stories about specific people better than names of entire communities or countries.

Client Profile. The client profile includes some of the same information as the case history, but has a different format. Profiles give more detail on the history and future plans of the person, group or company along with their names, faces and, possibly, phone numbers to contact. The profile includes how and why they use your products or services. The sales power of profiles is weaker than that of case histories.

Build rapport with your customers, members or supporters by using client profiles. Including a profile in each issue lets your readers know you appreciate their business or involvement. Show photographs of your clients as part of the recognition. For example, include a photograph along with an article on your best customer being voted woman of the year.

One consultant used her local newsletter as a way to help her clients "network" with each other. She included information on clients' services along with their phone numbers. Increasing business for your clients is a sure way to build customer loyalty.

Welcoming New Clients. Organizations with expanding client bases may include a welcome message along with a list of new clients or members. This not only recognizes the new customers, but tells existing clients that you are not resting on your laurels and are an active player in your industry. Caution may be necessary, though, to ensure that existing customers know you still value their business.

Providing Support for Customers

Another way to demonstrate commitment to your readers is to provide them with help and information. By giving your readers technical information and support through your newsletter, you'll increase the value of your publication. Support articles also help spur reader enactment. Within this type of article, you can reiterate the features of your products or services. You allay one of the greatest fears of most customers: you assure them they won't be abandoned after their purchase or decision to support you.

Support information can include:

> "how to" lists
> how to make better use of your products or services
> background information on an issue or current event
> educational material to help readers advance their careers
> worksheets to help readers save or budget money
> toll-free phone numbers for customers to call with questions
> tips for dealers on how to promote your products

Often, the support articles you provide for your customers save you time or money as well. For example, you can include an article or diagram showing the fastest way to call people within your company. By giving the exact exchange to dial, you can save your operators' time and avoided switchboard backlog.

If you are a manufacturer, you may be able to provide information that helps a customer prevent a problem. Such support articles include tips on installation, troubleshooting, maintenance and repair. You can also give assistance on product selection if you offer a broad product line.

Some companies are hesitant to discuss technical problems with their products. Of course, it's best to design a product and create documentation so there's never a problem. But, if there is one, you are better off solving it quickly and helping others to avoid it. You can easily include a standard support feature by gathering your support people together and pooling the most commonly asked questions during the last month or so. You can also solicit questions from readers and answer their letters in the newsletter. Telling readers that other people are asking these questions will encourage readers to save the newsletter in case they have the same problem.

The question and answer format is useful for commonly-asked questions. It allows readers to skim through the questions.

A cellular phone service included a support article telling readers how to avoid unproductive time while driving. The article discussed using cassette tapes, dictaphones and, of course, cellular phones. It provided another place to talk about the time management advantages of using a cellular phone.

Some manufacturers of complex products have so much technical information to provide customers that they choose to publish a special insert. The inserts can include special information such as page after page of programming codes that are of interest to some readers, but too technical for others.

Including support information in your newsletter saves you time and encourages readers to save the publication. Most importantly, it assures readers that you take care of your customers and supporters after their purchase or donation.

Including Your Organization's News

It's often a challenge to include your organization's news without appearing boastful. Along with articles detailing the specifics of your products or services, there are other ways of including your own news while keeping readers interested.

As with product articles, you have to show rather than tell. To show how your executives, members or doctors are capable administrators, list their industry activities. Include condensed versions of speeches, technical papers or seminars. Discuss upcoming trade shows and events your organization supports.

Articles by Experts. Show that your president or other officers keep abreast with your industry by having them write regular columns on general trends in your industry or on technical subjects. For example, if your product or service fits in with a topic that's been hot in the news, assign one of your executives to write an editorial. Examples that come to mind are computer viruses, safe packaging, recycling, acid rain and controversial books or movies. Every industry has several hot topics to choose from at any given time and these articles can also be forwarded to trade journals.

For example, the owner of a pool and spa store used an editorial format to discuss the various methods of cleaning a pool. The article was written and presented as an opinion. Within the editorial, the author promoted the types of cleaning products his company carried.

Provide a personalized, approachable image by including by-lines and photographs with all columns. Including photos can help the profile of regular columnists. People will recognize them at industry events.

Milestones. To demonstrate the stability of your organization, you can report on the milestones you've reached. Events such as the 100,000th unit shipped or your 25th anniversary are possibilities. Along with these milestones you can include some background on your organization. Within milestone articles, recognize your customers or supporters for making the event possible. This shifts the focus of the article from your organization to your customers.

Employee and Member Profiles. To show the capabilities of your new or existing staff, include profiles of employees or members. Print candid pictures alongside articles to attract attention.

Most customers want to see the people they're dealing with. Behind-the-scenes people can also make good profiles. Show how they help customers or contribute to the organization. Your customer may not be aware, for example, of the extremes your dispatch supervisor takes in finding trucking companies to deliver a shipment overnight. Because you always deliver on time, your customers assume it's easy. By focusing on the key employee, you give the employee recognition while showing customers how hard you work for them.

Unfortunately, some articles on employees aren't inherently interesting. Articles focusing on the personal accomplishments of your staff such as number of years with the company, babies born and classes attended aren't appropriate for most promotional newsletters. Leave them for your in-house publication.

Advertising. For organizations that want to include advertising in their publication, one option is to "report" it. Alert your customers or members to advertising or publicity appearing in trade journals. If an advertisement has been effective, include it in the newsletter. Add a commentary on why you feel it's doing well. You can also announce when you have new literature. Include a picture of the brochure or catalog. If you include an advertisement in your newsletter, separate it from the editorial material. Follow the guidelines of newspapers. Advertisements are clearly marked or boxed off. Any editorial material appearing on products or services is written in a news style.

Some companies list the public relations exposure they've received. By listing the publication, date and page number of the articles written on your organization, you might inspire your newsletter readers to search the journals for more information about you. It also shows that you are making important enough progress to warrant industry-wide coverage.

Awards or Achievements. Articles reporting on awards your organization has received are inherently dull. The only exception is when the award signifies a major achievement in the eyes of your readers.

> Another option for including advertisements is to reprint your ad in full color on glossy paper and use it as an insert.

Be cautious when reporting on awards received or given by your organization. Make sure they're really important, such as making the *Inc.* 500 list or something that's relevant to your customers' interest in your organization. They must be promotional to be worth reporting.

Grab Readers With Industry Summaries

Industry information is the "news" part of your newsletter. It's often the feature which draws readers—especially prospects—to your publication. Your newsletter may include news items quoted from industry publications. Include anything interesting you can find. Research findings, technology breakthroughs, pending legislation, opinions of prominent industry figures and information on other people's products are all good news items. Write the reports in your own words and list the publication and its date so that readers can look up the complete article if they desire.

Every organization has industry news to report. An investment house can report how changes in tax laws affect people with retirement plans. Politicians can inform voters on pending legislation or new taxpayer rights.

Reporting on research reflects well on your organization and increases the value of your newsletter. Even if you didn't conduct the research yourself, readers credit you with the expertise. Graphics add further credibility to reports.

The uniqueness of your publication lies not in providing timely news, but in compiling information of interest to your readers. This saves them from reading and assembling the same information from several publications. These news blurbs usually fall under headlines like "industry news" or "news briefs."

People read news summaries. In reader surveys for two different publications, the news features received the highest percentage of readership reaching 82% in one and 90% in the other. Because of high reader penetration, include a news blurb on your organization along with the others.

Longer industry articles report on trends, trade shows, technical meetings, seminars, assemblies, conventions, press tours, sales meetings and user groups. Keep in mind that many of your readers weren't at the trade show or meeting. Give them the benefit of having gone. Summarize the important new things you saw and learned. Your readers will thank you for saving them the trip.

IN THE NEWS

OEM Ties Push Unix to the Zenith

Demand for a standardized operating system, growing popularity of '386-based micros, the XENIX/UNIX merger and porting UNIX to the Apple Macintosh have combined to push AT&T's venerable operating system to the front in the PC marketplace.

As micro-based multi-user systems gained a stronghold in business, engineering and manufacturing applications, systems designers demanded more standardization, according to DigiBoard President John P. Schinas. Strategic alliances with OEMs such as Apple and IBM are also a sign that micro multi-user platforms will continue to grow in popularity, he added.

Pick Marketing PC Version

Pick Systems Inc. has set up a division to aggressively market the PC version of its Pick operating system through VARs and distributors, the company announced in early March.

Vice President of Sales and Marketing Frank Petyak said the company sold about 12,000 PC operating systems during the fiscal year ending February 29, and has set a goal to double sales of the operating system each year for the next three years.

IBM Gives Nod

In what one industry analyst called a "ringing endorsement for the UNIX workstation market", IBM has announced a new version of its AIX operating system for the RT PC, as well as enhancements to the unreleased AIX system for the PS/2 Model 80.

IBM Vice President Andrew Heller said these enhancements will give the RT and Model 80 more connectivity options than anything currently available for competing UNIX systems.

AIX Version 2.2, available for the RT in June, will support new communications software including enhancements to the UNIX networking standard TCP/IP and Systems Network Architecture (SNA) services.

IBM Drops Gloves Plans PS/2 Blitz

IBM officials in February disclosed an aggressive agenda calling for the release of as many as 11 new PS/2 models in 1988, also promising an extensive new line of support hardware including high-resolution graphics boards and high-capacity hard drives.

The company also said it will cut prices on existing PS/2s, with the '286-based Models 50 and 60 selling for approximately $1,350 by late 1988. A '386 machine at that price point was hinted at by the end of 1989.

Industry watchers call the price cuts a dramatic shift away from IBM's traditional high-margin marketing strategy.

Flashbacks From the IMTEC Show

If several of your customers attend the same trade show, include their photos along with quick descriptions of them. Unlike the focus in which you only cover one company, this allows you to give recognition to several customers at once.

Another way to cover a variety of clients or members at once is to report on an industry trend. Quote several different people and include their photographs. By doing your own interviews, you may end up with an angle not covered by trade publications. This will grab the attention not only of your readers, but also of the news editors on your mailing list. If you receive any interesting letters as a result, publish them as letters to the editor (only after securing the author's permission; letters are covered under copyright law).

Materials for Appliances

Washington Penn Plastic is currently developing a product line of calcium carbonate and talc filled polypropylenes for appliance applications. Many products currently have UL approval and several others will have it by the end of the year. In addition, many products are also being tested to be in compliance with FDA regulations.

Polypropylene compounds are currently being used or being tested for the following major appliance applications:

washers — outer tubs, inner tubs, splash rings, motor housings
dishwashers– door liners, tubs, rack wheels, motor housings
refrigerators–door and food liners
dryers– blower fans

Sidebar.

One manufacturer reported on the cost-cutting measures being taken in the appliance industry. Because the company manufactures cost-saving replacement materials, a sidebar listing its products was included within the article. Even within your news reporting, never miss an opportunity to promote yourself.

Reader's Service Items Increase Response

Some information is compiled for the sole benefit of your readers. It includes lists of events, book reviews and philosophical pieces offering helpful techniques on management or self-motivation. Even though most of this information isn't promotional, make sure it has some relevance to your organization.

One manufacturer included reader service information on how to use statistics to improve the quality of manufactured goods. As an illustration within the article, the editor used her own company. As a result, readers were educated about quality improvements while also learning about the publisher's quality control program. The editor seized an opportunity to sneak in promotional material with no loss of reader interest.

You can also boost reader response by offering a free reprint of an interesting article, a free product sample or a premium. You can offer an annual index of articles along with a form to request back issues (often appreciated by new readers).

Some newsletters include contests, questions, trivia or other methods of attracting readers' interest. A data processing company stores information for companies on magnetic tape, called fiche. Every issue has a trivia question about fiche. In one issue, readers had to estimate the miles of paper saved by storing information electronically. Each person entering a guess received a luggage tag and the winner won a travel bag. The publisher made the contest fun while also reaffirming one of the ecological benefits of using their services.

Coupons also benefit readers by saving them money. Usually, lower ticket items are more appropriate for a coupon than more expensive ones. A coupon for a free item or money off the customer's next purchase outpulls coupons requiring an additional purchase. Always state the expiration date—sooner for low budget items and later for high priced ones. Clearly indicate any restrictions. Inform your representatives of the coupon and make sure all of your regular clients receive it.

A landscape supplier included coupons in his gardening publication. One of the goals of the newsletter was to increase traffic into the nursery. To entice readers, they included a coupon for a free plant. To help reduce inventory, he also included a coupon for 10% off non-plant items. The coupons do double-duty—they catch those looking for plants as well as those who like to do it themselves and only want supplies.

To retain the integrity of your newsletter and keep it from looking like a sales piece, the offers included should be viewed as a service to readers. You can offer informative items such as free literature, buyer's guides, reprints of speeches or technical papers, videos or slide presentations.

By including helpful information, you encourage readers to save the publication. When readers save your newsletter, they might even read your promotional material a second time.

How it All Comes Together

Most newsletters contain a mixture of the six types of articles. Mix and match the various types depending on your promotional needs. Coupons are useful for increasing traffic into your business. Case histories reassure first time buyers or supporters. Employee profiles and company editorials make your staff more approachable, and so on.

To give you a feel for what the mixture might look like, study the newsletter published by a music store. The store wanted to increase sales by announcing new products. To convince readers of the expertise of the store's sales staff, the newsletter includes employee profiles showing that each person is a musical expert. Support articles, a brief list of hard-to-find items, and announcements of upcoming seminars give the newsletter added value. Each of these articles strives toward the same goal: to increase business at the store.

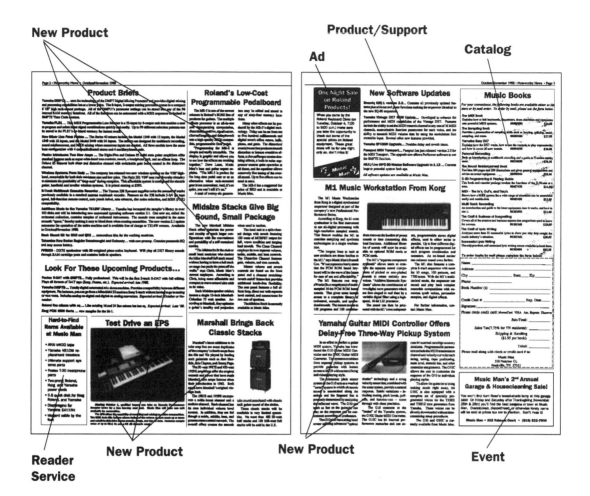

Other publishers concentrate on one specific method per issue for achieving their goals. These are called theme issues. For example, an association's theme issue may center around its annual membership drive. The issue could include event calendars, a message from national headquarters, and a page full of member testimonials along with photographs.

If you're announcing a new product or service, you can mention it several times in your newsletter. Include an announcement in the industry news section. Devote an entire article to the new product or service on a different page. Insert a reprint of the ad you're running in industry publications.

Many professional associations hold annual seminars and events. The main event for one association is a half-day workshop followed by an afternoon of golf. The group strives to get 80 percent of its membership to sign up. The event is the group's top fund raiser.

Though the workshop topics change from year to year, the event is usually remembered by the competitive game of golf that follows. To assure that no one forgets, the association president published reminders of the event in the six newsletters leading up to the outing. Each reminder used the same graphic of a golf club. In the issue just prior to the event, the golf club was used on the cover, on the schedule, and on the seminar description. The constant reminder plus the use of a consistent graphic increased attendance to over 90 percent.

Do You Need Multiple Newsletters?

The mixture of content discussed so far assumes you can reach all of your readers with the same newsletter. For some types of organizations, this is not possible. To be more effective, some editors produce more than one version of their newsletter.

If your organization has more than one area of expertise, consider doing more than one newsletter or producing several versions of the same one. This allows you to target the various markets you serve. For example, many raw material suppliers sell to several different industries. A vinyl manufacturer may sell to the PVC pipe extrusion industry, the vinyl siding extrusion market, the wire and cable industry, and the special purpose vinyl marketplace. This manufacturer could have four different newsletters or could have a section in one newsletter devoted to providing information for each market.

The same is true for other organizations such as banks and hospitals. Both find their clients to have specialized needs depending on their age. Young adults are having babies and buying new homes. Middle-aged people are trying to stay healthy, send their children to college, and plan for retirement. People who are older may live on a fixed budget and often need specialized care. Savvy marketers of banks and hospitals are sending out newsletters targeting each of these age groups.

Many companies sell their products directly to the end user, while others may also sell to dealers and distributors. Depending on the distribution structure for your products and services, you may want to create separate publications for each of these customer segments.

You can also design a publication for your dealers to mail to their own clients. By helping your dealers market themselves, you will increase your business in turn. Be sure to leave space on the newsletter for the dealer to customize it with a photo, address, ad, logo or article.

Companies with offices in several different areas can customize their newsletter for each of the territories. Many realty firms do this. An industrial controls distributor used this approach for eight representatives throughout the Southeast. They printed the sales representative's photograph on the cover and a personalized message on the back. This further enhanced the readers' feelings of being called on personally by their representative.

Reaching All Your Markets With Inserts

Another way to reach market segments is through inserts. Design a standard four page newsletter and insert one specialized page. Your ability to use inserts depends on how specifically you can sort your list. You may code your list based on the types of products your customers buy, or by organization. Another way to segment your readers is by the experience they have with your organization. For example, you may use a standard insert to welcome new customers and members. The insert could show pictures and descriptions of your staff, details on your policies, or special background information.

In the pilot issue of your newsletter, you may want to insert a letter from your president or marketing manager introducing the publication. If you rent mailing lists, you may want to include a letter explaining why the new readers are receiving the publication.

> If your organization serves more than one specific market, consider special inserts for each segment. A computer dealer, for example, can use an insert to target publishing, legal and healthcare markets. The editor can sort the mailing list by market type and only send the legal insert to lawyers, for example.

Like the songwriters' cafe, you can use the insert page to publish a calendar. Make sure the calendar is easily removed. Take care not to have important items, like the continuation of an article, on the reverse side.

Including an insert in your newsletter is an inexpensive way to squeeze additional mileage out of your publication. After all, you're already paying a fixed amount for postage (up to a certain weight). It makes sense to "piggyback" more information.

Within the content of your newsletter, you can piggyback more than inserts. Some distributors include a catalog within the body of the newsletter. These newsletter/catalog hybrids are called newsalogs. Newsalogs function as both a newsletter and a catalog.

Readers are drawn to the piece by its helpful information. The front page contains lead articles just as newsletters do. As readers thumb through, they reach product descriptions and ordering information. This format allows publishers to detail products and provide helpful information for selecting and using the items.

Syndicated Newsletters Save Time & Money

You may not need to generate all original content. A syndicated newsletter may be available for your industry.

You probably already receive some syndicated newsletters. Syndicated (or franchised) newsletters are mass-produced for specific markets. Common users are doctors, banks, chiropractors and accountants. These organizations buy newsletters pre-written by someone else. The same newsletter is sold to other organizations in other areas of the country.

Most syndicated newsletter companies offer their clients exclusivity within zip code areas in order to eliminate the possibility of competitors sending the same publication to identical prospects. Many of these services leave room for their clients to customize them by printing their names and sometimes their pictures on the front or back cover.

You may have already received promotional material from a syndicated newsletter supplier. If not, check with the national headquarters of your professional association. The research department should have names of syndicated newsletters for your industry. Many professional associations have entered the syndicated newsletter field. For example, the American Academy of Ophthalmology offers members a publication called *Your Vision*. Magazine publishers have jumped on the bandwagon, too. *Practical Accountant* magazine offers *Client's Monthly Alert*.

There are several advantages to using a syndicated newsletter service. You can produce a quality product without having any editorial and design experience. It saves you the time you would have had to spend researching, writing, editing and producing a newsletter. The overall cost is usually lower because syndicated newsletters benefit from the economy of larger print runs. They can also spread out editorial and production costs. In addition to saving you money, you are freed from the time and burden of production.

Several different syndicated services are offered for banks and other financial institutions. The Signal Group, in Nashville, TN, for example, offers banks several services. Banks can purchase either completed newsletters or use of articles and photographs for their in-house managed publications. The company has even expanded the concept to radio and offers a series of personalized 60-second financial tips.

On the other hand, there are also important advantages to producing the newsletter yourself. Your own publication has more of a personal touch. You have complete control of the content and can better match the newsletter to your current marketing goals and your client profile. By self-publishing you can also set your own schedule and change the size, length or graphic design to fit your needs.

An alternative is to combine the benefits of syndicated newsletters with those of self-publishing. You can use a syndicated newsletter but personalize it by enclosing a note. You can include an insert page of news unique to your organization and clients. When you do this, try to match the graphic "feel" so it appears to come from a single source.

Often syndicated newsletter services will customize a version of their standard newsletter for you. They can include an article submitted by you targeting your specific readers. Or they may let you purchase only the articles and use them in your own newsletter.

If you decide to publish your own newsletter, consider franchising it. Sell it to businesses similar to yours in other areas. This is how many syndicated newsletters get started. Since you're already going through the steps of publishing your own newsletter, your organization may want to turn it into a profit-generating venture.

A book store owner has done this with her newsletter. Now, in addition to her store, she operates Book News Publications. She publishes four issues per year of *BookNews* and *Kids' Line*. Over 70 other bookstores buy her publication.

Content: Covering your tracks

Whether you generate all of the content yourself, or utilize a news service, you are legally responsible for what is printed in your newsletter. To conclude the discussion on content, heed a few warnings.

Whenever you publish a news piece, you are opening yourself up to a certain degree of liability. If you let this bother you too much, you'll publish a stilted, boring newsletter. Caution is necessary, however, to assure your publication promotes rather than harms client relations. For this reason, let's discuss some of the potential problems with newsletter content.

Libel. If you publish an article, statement or piece of art that injures a person's reputation, is false, or is in reckless disregard of the truth, you can be sued for libel. If you have to print this type of material, verify all names and facts, and if you are unsure about an item, do not print it.

In a promotional newsletter, stick to more positive information. Avoid printing any potentially defamatory information. This doesn't mean you can't include controversial stories; just be sure you represent the facts in a fair, unbiased, and accurate manner free from personal attacks.

Disclaimers. If you are carrying professional advice in your newsletter, consult your lawyer. Request an appropriate disclaimer to place in each issue. Such a disclaimer might read, "Information provided in this newsletter is general in nature and should not be relied upon to solve any particular situation."

While you want your newsletter to be helpful, you don't want your readers to rely solely on the information contained in the newsletter. Try, wherever possible, to encourage readers to call for complete information.

Letting the Competition Know. There's a problem with keeping your prospects well informed of your activities and new products. You run the risk of your competition seeing the publication and finding out, too.

The benefits of spreading your organization's news far outweigh these drawbacks. The exposure and increased sales gained by educating readers outweigh any losses occurred from competitors seeing your products.

Publishing a newsletter is a lot like teaching. When you teach others, you always learn more about the subject in the process. Instead of having your "students" catch up with you, you advance even further.

9

Research Brings Writing Success

Contrary to what you may be fearing, it won't take you years to learn to write in a way that attracts readers. Your writing success hinges on how well you clearly present quality, condensed information. You already have the skills it takes to write an effective newsletter article—the ability to research and organize ideas. Develop your writing style at your own pace.

After you choose the content for each issue, it's time to put on your archaeologist's hat. Instead of ancient ruins, your dig is for interesting information that promotes your organization. Your readers want diamonds. You want results.

With shovel in hand, plow through the mounds of information. Once you unearth valuable facts, sift through them and save the most precious ones. Pocket them in your safari shorts. Rattle them around for awhile. Then, you're ready to inscribe them in your scrolls. The deeper you've dug, and the finer your sifting screen, the more you rattle, the less time it takes to inscribe. Dig. Sift. Rattle. Inscribe. Grab your spade. You'll look great in khaki.

Where to Dig for Facts

Research requires more time to complete than writing. When you first break ground on a new issue, draw a research map. Think about who would know or care about your particular subject. More importantly, who would benefit by helping you get the information in print. It's important to think this through. A research map leads you to the best treasures as quickly as possible.

Start with sources close to home. Search out experts in your own camp. Talk to members, doctors, salespeople, engineers, fund raisers and so on. Your beat could also include other organizations or industry experts. Request information and ask if they've seen a similar article in a recent publication. Someone may even have an entire file on the subject.

If you're writing about a service or product, collect any marketing materials already written. Brochures and fliers are helpful because they already include benefits and reasons for buying.

Keep in mind other sources for specialists. Consult the *Encyclopedia of Associations* to see if there's a special interest group on the subject. *Editor & Publisher International Yearbook* can provide you with the names of writers to interview. For instance, say you are writing an article for a travel agency newsletter about touring by motorcycle. You've noticed more older people on motorcycles and wonder if it's a trend. Call the public relations department of Harley-Davidson or Honda to see if they have statistics on their buyers. Call *Cycle* magazine to see if they have information. Visit a local motorcycle dealer.

When writing about a broader subject, dig deeper. If you have time, hike over to the library. Most periodical listings are computerized now. Enter the subject name you're researching and see how many magazine sources you find. For newsletters, magazine articles are usually more current than books. The information has already been sifted, too, since there's limited space in most periodicals.

When soliciting information from other people, send along a copy of your newsletter (or a sample sketch if it doesn't yet exist). This gives the writer a better understanding of what you're looking for. Provide a maximum word count so their material fits the allocated space.

Express Digging—Using Existing Material

As the leader of your newsletter project, it's important for you to know some fact-finding shortcuts. Whether you write the articles yourself or subcontract them, sifting through looser soil saves you money.

You don't have to generate 100% original material for each issue. If you find a jewel in a trade journal, newsletter or news wire service, ask for permission to reprint it. Solicit articles from vendors, customers, members and industry experts. Just make sure they're of strong interest to your readers and that they satisfy the goals of your publication.

Although some writers charge a fee for using their material, many people—industry experts and even professional writers—contribute material for free. Their motives are varied. Some want publicity. Some enjoy seeing their names and thoughts in print. Others are sincerely eager to make contributions to their fields.

To generate interest, publish open invitations for contributors in your newsletter. Explain how to submit an article. Place this in the masthead or elsewhere in the newsletter. Something like "Contributions welcome" will do.

The only potential problem with accepting contributions is that you often encounter bad writers. And the writers with less experience or skill seem to be most sensitive when their article is rewritten, cut or rejected. (It's no accident that good writers are interested in how you changed or improved their writing.) Avoid offending contributors. Call them and discuss your policy of editing articles to fit the tone of your publication and the space available.

Readers Send in the Gems

If you regularly include articles on clients and members, solicit information in advance. Send out letters to all of your readers requesting information on their organizations. This gives everyone an equal opportunity to appear in the newsletter. It also provides you with a response to any charges of favoritism.

Soliciting information accelerates you into the sifting stage. Sort through the information you receive and choose the most interesting items. Contact the organizations to collect further data and to interview for quotes.

While it's important to use the news of others, don't forget to use your own organization's press releases. If public relations is handled in a department different from yours, ask to be added to the media list. This not only saves writing time, it adds continuity to your marketing and public relations efforts.

You can design a standard form for each newsletter. An alumni publication uses this to gather information from members.

We need Alumni Personals!

Use this handy form to send us news about you and yours ! The item(s) will be printed in the next issue of the Newsletter. We Promise!

To Susan Mullin Toutant
10200 Statia Lynn Court
Louisville, Ky 40223

Here's a news item about _____

_____

Class of _____

_____

_____

_____

_____

Interested in becoming a Class Represenative? _____

The Idea File Saves Back-Tracking

Like any good archaeologist, tagging and storing your artifacts is important. Your backlog can come in handy.

As you're thinking about each newsletter (or even between issues), you'll uncover information for future issues. Other times, you may have "spillover" information you couldn't fit in your current publication.

Safely store these fragments from your dig, along with all necessary reference information, in an "idea file." Ideas can also be kept in a loose leaf binder. Binders are helpful for noting and tracking thoughts that surface in editorial board meetings.

Your stash of ideas is not only helpful for the next issue, it can also save you during disasters. In case an article isn't ready at the deadline, something in your idea file can fill the gap. Having current information in your idea file, though, is often a challenge. Some industries such as medical, computer and insurance change rapidly. If an article is more than six months old, it's out of date. Try to keep an up-to-date safety net on hand. If you're using a desktop publishing system, have the articles written and stored on your computer. If you take your copy to a typesetter, have the articles typeset and ready to paste down.

Government Property & Other Information

The government is actively involved in gathering a variety of information. Before you embark on a dig, see if the information is already available from a government office. Write or call the Government Printing Office in Washington D.C. for more information.

If you have a computer equipped with a modem, you have an electronic shovel. You can tap into electronic news services, databases and bulletin boards. A complete list of news services is listed in Appendix B and includes those for financial, legal, medical, legislative, education, business and science and technology information.

You can also swap information with other newsletter publishers. Though this is more common with non-profit organizations, you may have a willing editor in your industry.

Digging for Industry News in Copyrighted Lands

A less formal method of sharing is by researching the writing of others. Read your industry publications. Clip all of the articles related to your particular service or product. Sift and summarize the news for your readers. Note trends and write them up in brief articles.

Another method of making a page inviting is by using short news blurbs. Newsbriefs condense long articles into two or three lines. This gives readers the feeling they're merely skimming the headlines.

The short news items you uncover can be grouped together under headings such as "Newsbriefs," "In the News," and so on. Condense related material under one heading to reduce repetition. Weed out unnecessary words to give skimmers a feeling of "compartmentalization." List the magazines or other sources you use to create the newsbrief. It keeps you out of copyright violation and helps readers who want more information on the subject.

While reading industry publications, keep an eye out for useful ideas and information. While you cannot quote directly from others' copyrighted publications, you can use the information offered. A copyright protects a given combination of words, but does not give any exclusive rights to the information or ideas presented by those words. Industry ethics, however, state that you should list sources especially when using the information for promotion.

When using other articles, you can either summarize the article in your own words ("reporting" on the article) or you can reprint the article with permission. Using quotes is permissible up to an ambiguous point. Then, it becomes copyright infringement. A few sentences is safe. Fair usage laws state that you may quote briefly from a copyright work for purposes of criticism, comment, news reporting, teaching, scholarship or research. Your use of copyrighted material in a newsletter falls under news reporting rather than research.

The amount you can quote without permission is difficult to establish. The law states that the portion quoted can't be a substantial portion of the copyrighted work. It also can't significantly affect the market value of the work. When quoting from a copyrighted work, cite the title, publisher and publication date.

To use copyrighted information in a way not covered by fair usage law, request a written release from the owner. To determine who holds the copyright, look in the masthead (in a magazine or newsletter) or on the page after the title page in a book. Photographs will usually carry a stamp at the bottom or on the back.

Send a form along with a copy of your newsletter and a photocopy of the material you want to use. Most people will grant permission free of charge. In some instances, though, you may have to pay for it. Unless otherwise specified, the fee is for one-time use only.

If you see an article you'd like to use that's written about a specific organization, call the featured company directly. Chances are that the article came from one of their news releases. Request a copy of the release. Contact the person listed on the release to get the rest of the story—more details or maybe a "story behind the story." The result will be a piece far more interesting and significant than the original release.

Many organizations and companies will send you photographs, catalogs, drawings and other useful items including complete press kits. The implication is that you are free to use them in your newsletter. However, few of those who send you that material also send you written permission. Be safe. Send them a release form like the one below.

Material that is not copyrighted is referred to as public domain. Most clip art is an example of public domain. Most everything else is copyrighted. Use the previous form to solicit written releases for everything else you use in your newsletter (letters from customers, for example). If you reprint a letter that wasn't intended as a letter to the editor, you must obtain permission. The author of the letter owns the copyright.

Cartoons and poems are often the most tempting to use without permission. Other people's writing isn't as tempting because you can always rewrite it and often want to anyway. Read on to see why you shouldn't use your favorite cartoon without permission.

Request to Reprint Material

The following material has caught our attention and we'd like to reprint it in our newsletter. Please sign this form and return it using the enclosed envelope.

We look forward to receiving your permission and giving your material greater exposure. Please indicate the acknowledgement you wish to appear along with your work in the newsletter.

Material to be Reprinted:

Title: _____

Author: _____

Copyright Date & Holder: _____

Permission Granted by: _____ Date: _____

Acknowledgement to read: _____

Publication Your Material Is to be Reprinted In:

Newsletter Name: _____

Publisher: _____

Address: _____

_____

Phone #: _____

Contact: _____

Thank you for your prompt response.

Using Copyrighted Material Without Permission In copyrightland, asking for forgiveness rather than permission is expensive. Under current laws, statutory damages of at least $250 per copy have been set. This means that if 2,000 copies of your newsletter are printed, the copyright owner will be entitled to a minimum of $250 x 2,000 or $500,000, plus legal fees.

Copyrighting Your Own Publication. You can copyright your newsletter by including the statement "Copyright or © + year + name of individual and/or organization." This doesn't register your copyright with the Copyright Office of the Library of Congress. If someone plagiarizes your material and you wish to take legal action, as part of filing suit you must register the copyright by using a form available from the Copyright Office, Library of Congress, Washington, DC 20559.

Most publishers of free newsletters see no particular value in barring others from borrowing their information. In fact, it often results in free publicity. Some organizations copyright the publication and print a notice in the masthead advising readers they are free to copy and republish anything in the newsletter, as long as they credit the source.

While you can copyright the content of your newsletter, you can't copyright its name. The closest you can come is by trademarking the name's graphic design as it appears in your nameplate.

Dialing for Artifacts

The information for your newsletter isn't limited by other written sources. It's often as close as the telephone. Some of the most interesting facts aren't written up in a report or in a magazine article. So, put down your shovel and pick up the phone.

Quotes add interest and newsworthiness to a story. They can transform a story about anything—a building, a product, a political system—into a story about people.

This is why interviewing is so important. You can interview someone for background information or as part of a personality profile. When interviewing for background information, keep the focus of your article in mind. Do your own research first and use quotes to clarify or rebut what is generally known. Sometimes you will determine the article's focus after the interview. In this case, don't be shy about calling up for additional information.

I live in New Orleans and recently took some friends visiting from France to a nearby plantation. The house itself was a disappointment. It could have been a disaster.

Instead, we were led through the house by an experienced guide. She relayed stories that other tourists had told her. For example, she told us that women used to shield their faces from the fire with fans. Their complexions were usually pock marked from diseases. So, they smoothed their skin with wax. If they got too close to the fire, their faces would actually melt!

The hour-long tour through the house was one interesting story after the other. This woman was an expert at making stories out of facts. By using information from other people, she took a rundown plantation and brought it to life.

Quotes also inject another "voice" into your writing, giving a variety in the style and sentence structure of the piece. Sometimes this other voice can be used to put in blatant sales pitches that would otherwise reduce the credibility of your article. Quote your sales manager's description of the product. The sales manager can be quoted as saying the "best" or "fastest," but you shouldn't write this type of subjective information outside of quotes.

If you only have one question to ask someone, just pick up the phone and call. If you're writing an entire article about someone or their opinions, arrange a formal interview. With a few rules of thumb, your job as an interviewer can be easy.

A Road Map to Good Interviewing

As an editor, one of your jobs is to promote your publication to other people. You're forever building bridges. You want to develop a list of contacts to call on whenever you're in need. Pretend contributors are people with nice homes in the mountains and you want to make sure you're invited back. You first let them know you're coming. While you're there, be as polite as possible. And, after you're back home, you send a thank you note and maybe even a small gift.

Assure future cooperation with interviewees the same way. Send a copy of the publication ahead of time. Have the person send you materials such as brochures including the description and history to shorten the interview time and to help prompt questions. Arrange an appointment for the interview, even if it's going to be held over the phone. Think of questions ahead of time. Your list should be painstakingly generated. If interview questions are dull and abstract, the answers will be too.

Once your interview begins, a few tips can make your visit fun and pleasant. Before you start asking questions, reassure the subject that they'll be the first to approve the article before anyone else sees it. Also, ask how many copies of the printed newsletter they'd like to receive.

To get things off on the right foot, set the person at ease. Smile, even if you're on the phone. People can "hear" a smile through your conversational tone of voice. If interviewing in person, don't take out your notebook right away. Once the person begins to smile or laugh, the interview flows much easier. Start with easy questions like, "What is your title and the correct spelling of your name?" Even if it's a common name, always verify the spelling. Remember, even Smith has variations. Misprinted names and titles are embarrassing.

Make the person feel interesting. Listen carefully to the interviewee for hints of follow-up questions to ask. If you don't understand something, ask. "What does that stand for?" "What do you mean?" "Why was that?" Most people are understanding if you explain to them that you are new to an industry and need help with the jargon. They aren't forgiving, however, if you haven't done your homework (the busier the person, the more unforgiving). When interviewing people with more responsibilities, cut right to the important questions. Get basic information from their assistants.

If the person strays from your list of questions and you like the new direction, let it happen.

Fill in your notes immediately after the interview while the subject is fresh in your mind. It's easy to forget many of the interview's details once a few days go by. For telephone interviews, either type or hand-write notes. Develop you own system of abbreviations, especially for terms common to your industry.

If you're concerned about catching all of the person's quotes, find out if it's okay to tape the interview. If using a tape recorder, take notes as well. You'll often write down a follow-up question while the person continues to talk. Set the counter on the recorder to "0" beforehand. When the person says something you know you'll use, jot down where on the tape the quote occurs. This saves you from listening to the entire tape. Assure the person being taped that no one will hear the tape but you.

When writing your article, sift quotes, too. Use only the best words. Paraphrase and condense other thoughts within the text of the article. Take care to present the opinions and thoughts of the interviewee accurately. You can rearrange the order of quotes only if they don't change in meaning.

> "I was interviewing the national marketing director of a Fortune 500 company. The interview never got off the ground. I used the same format as I had for smaller companies. I was asking the easiest questions first, trying to put him at ease. He became progressively angry. He finally told me to contact the PR department for this basic information. He didn't have time. He said not to call back until I'd done my homework."

Avoid writing up interviews in question and answer style. Quotations are livelier when they pop up within a well-organized article.

After you've written the article, it's time to check back in with your host. Before starting production, have the person read over the article. Few people make extensive changes and invariably they find a misspelled name or other potentially embarrassing mistakes. With the popularity of facsimile machines, you can probably send the article electronically. Have the interviewee send the changes back the same way. To avoid misunderstandings, don't take changes verbally. In case there's ever a question about something you've written, you will want the original information on file. An accurate article reflects well on your organization.

Once the article is in print, send a thank you note along with the number of extra copies the person wanted. If you interview several people per issue, keep their names and addresses together on a separate sheet of paper. Once your newsletter is printed, you'll have this at hand instead of buried within your notes. If you follow the majority of these steps, interviewees will find you professional and easy to work with. You're a shoe-in for that next visit to the mountains.

One last note. It's important to maintain a positive, professional attitude while conducting interviews. Many people are warm, talkative and a pleasure to interview. Unfortunately, some people aren't as willing. Remember your research plan. Find those who will benefit from being in your newsletter. They will be more helpful than someone with nothing to gain.

If someone seems uncooperative, try your best to discover the problem. Let the person know at the beginning of the interview that they can refuse to answer any question that makes them uncomfortable. If they continue to be unresponsive, ask, "Is this a bad time to call?" or "Would you rather not be interviewed for this publication?"

If you are interviewing in person and plan to bring a camera, let the person know. The interviewee may want to dress for the occasion or may need to request permission from someone else.

It's better for them, your company, and especially *you*, if you cut off the interview. Bad interviews make you hesitant to pick up the phone again. Remember, interesting and friendly people are still out there. Interviewing is a vital part of keeping your newsletter lively and well-read.

Protect yourself at all cost and keep interviewing a fun part of writing.

Sifting With a Promotional Screen

Uncover all the information you have time to find. This is usually two to three times the information you actually need. Then, you're ready to sift. The article you ultimately write will be packed with information aimed at your specific audience. In order to pack your article tightly, extract the essence. And, in order to customize it to your audience, you need a promotional filter.

The way you achieve this conciseness is independent of writing style. Before you sit down with pen in hand, sift through the information you've uncovered. Rank all bits in order of interest to your readers. Study the top items and see how your promotional material relates to it. Choose the focus of the article based on your promotional objectives. How do you want your reader to react after reading the article? Inspire them to request more information, volunteer, donate or buy. Or, leave them knowing more about your products and services than they did before.

For example, suppose your organization provides support for children with cerebral palsy. You've researched an article on one of your donors, Mrs. Smith, and found that one of her children has cerebral palsy. Mrs. Smith works at the hospital as a physical therapist. She loves to garden, she traveled to Europe last year to trace her family history, and she spends her free time studying languages.

Since your newsletter's subject is the importance of helping children with cerebral palsy, you would keep Mrs. Smith on that subject during the interview. Ask her to tell you stories about how she helps her child overcome the handicap. Find out exactly why she supports your organization. Ask her to talk about the handicap from a physical therapist's point of view. Learn what the reputation of your organization is among the other professionals at the hospital. Use the gardening and travel information as secondary information or to form a theme for the article.

Pull out the combination of facts and quotes from the other information you've gathered about Mrs. Smith. List them all on one sheet of paper. Within this list, rank the items in order of interest to your reader. Since not all your gems can fit, be prepared to leave some behind. If the organization of the article immediately takes shape and you catch yourself starting to write, go ahead.

Otherwise, taking care that you've transcribed all of your notes into legible form and assuming you have a bit of time, put them in your "pocket" and let them rattle around.

The Art of Rattling

Rattling helps you clear your thoughts and put your facts in order. Clear thinking becomes clear writing. Collect your artifacts as soon as the newsletter content is decided. If you wait too long, you won't have time to rattle.

Rattling isn't done consciously. Common places for rattling are in traffic, in the show, or while cleaning or exercising. You may have your own rattling time. You don't have to confess when.

It's important to realize the difference between rattling and procrastinating. If you're under a tight deadline and you're rattling, then, yes, it's procrastinating. But, if you have time, rattling usually improves the organization of your article and shortens writing time. Most people can research in a noisy environment, but few can write in one. You save time by uncovering all your artifacts, documenting them, then waiting for quiet moments to inscribe.

The most important rules for rattling are to collect and write down all the information you need to create the article. From there, your brain starts to work.

As your deadline approaches, sit down in a quiet room at your computer or with sharpened pencils and start writing your newsletter.

Good writing comes from uncovering interesting information and truly being excited about sharing it with other people.

10
Words That Elevate Climbers

Every word you write should be the best for capturing your reader's attention. This is an active role that requires your abundant promotional energy. As a writer, your challenge is to minimize the distance between you and your readers until you're acting as their personal guide.

When writing out a path for your prospects, start with the enactment level and work backwards to recognition. First, decide what action you want readers to take as a result of reading the article. Then, list the most interesting items and benefits readers receive by reading the article. Give readers the specific information they need to know in order to make a purchasing decision. Catch the skimmers by relaying your promotional points through the headline, leading sentence, photograph captions, pull quotes, kickers and subheads.

Once you've finished writing the articles, you must carefully word your contents box or teasers on the front or back cover to convince readers to open the publication.

This chapter is dedicated to promoting through specifics. But don't let allotted space communicate importance. All four levels of RISE—recognition, image, specifics and enactment—are of equal importance. If you have to ignore any one of the levels because of writing deadlines, make it the specifics. You can squeeze in a lot of promoting in your headlines, subheads, captions, teasers and other short blocks of words.

Start With Enactment

As a part of the "sifting" phase, you ask yourself, " What do I hope readers will do after reading this article? What do I want them to remember? How do I want them to feel?" This information needs to be added somewhere in the newsletter. Often it is placed at the end of the article in what's called a signature line. In most publications, signature lines identify the author of an article. In promotional newsletters they contain information such as where to call for more information or where to send orders or donations.

The conclusion of your articles should tell readers what to do—order today, write your legislator, come to the meeting.

Refer readers to a reply card if it's one of your desired responses. Reply cards give readers an opportunity to tell you they're interested. They can request more information, a product demonstration, a phone call, a sales visit— whatever method you choose. At the same time, you can solicit some information about potential customers. You can ask readers to tell you how they intend to use your product, when they plan to buy, or what products they are currently using. This information allows you to qualify leads and separate non-prospects from serious potential customers.

Repeat the benefit of replying on the card. Motivating readers to look at the reply card is part of the battle. Then you have to convince them to send it in. Put your message big and bold on your reply card. "Yes! I want to learn more about planning for a comfortable retirement. Send information about your retirement fund."

For donations, the reply card should repeat again why the donation is important. "I agree that my support is necessary to help the individuals who need hope in order to become self-sufficient," or, to affirm interest, "Tell me more about your products. I understand there is no cost or obligation to find out more. I am interested in the following items…"

If you're providing free information to readers, try to solicit at least one piece of information back from them that you can use to understand your prospects better.

Your reply card could be the same each issue. It could merely state "Please send me more information on…" and follow with a list of your products or services. Though it will save on printing, because you can pre-print the cards for several issues to come, it's better to have each reply card contain a special offer.

The reply card can urge readers to respond immediately. "Take advantage of this special offer. Mail today!" Use some exclamation marks. If printing in two colors, put the action text in the highlight color. Make the card *move*. "Special Offer!" "Yes! Reserve my subscription today." "We Don't Want Your Money. Order now and we'll bill you later. It's that easy!"

For more action, call it a *response* card instead of a reply card.

Include your telephone number in bold characters on the reply card in case the reader is inspired to take immediate action. Or include your fax number and encourage readers to send the card via facsimile versus mailing it.

Subjects That Attract Readers' Attention

You have to match the right article subject to the desired reader action. The article must be something your readers will pay attention to. Some subjects always attract readers. Take the word *survey* for example. "We recently surveyed customers and asked questions about their future plans. This is what they said…" Readers' ears immediately perk up. The answers to "common questions" generate a similar response.

How to save money is another universal desire. For example, "How to Save Money on Your Car Insurance." Almost everyone is interested in this topic. Studies show that the 16 most promotional words are:

➤ you/your	➤ love	➤ free
➤ fun	➤ money	➤ save
➤ results	➤ new	➤ health
➤ easy	➤ proven	➤ safe
➤ guarantee	➤ benefit	➤ how to
➤ now		

In moderation, work these words into your article headlines.

Your articles should deal directly with your readers' self-interest. Relate your message to your reader's area of responsibility. Talk sales to a sales manager, results to a donor, specifications to an engineer, benefits to a member, and profits to a president.

Once you've discovered this information, decide the best format for the article. To promote through specifics, you have to illustrate why readers should let your organization solve their problems. Support claims through guarantees, explanations, testimonials, case histories, free trials, test results or comparisons with competing products. The three main writing formats to use are news, feature and editorial.

Format for Late-Breaking News

The news format is used for announcements, to report trends, and for new product and service introductions. For promotional newsletters, approach the news format with caution. It encourages you to write in a way that keeps readers on the path for only a few steps.

News articles are usually written using an inverted pyramid format. The inverted pyramid is a method of organization used by newspapers in which the answers to the questions who, what, where, when, why and how are given first. It has its roots in the American Civil War when reporters filing stories by telegraph feared that the lines might be cut at any point during the transmission.

A news story starts with the climax, with details following in diminishing order of importance to readers until all the elaborating facts have been given. The story finally ends with the least significant information in the last paragraph. Thus, an article may be shortened from the end without losing much.

What's wrong with this? First, if you answer questions in the order of who, what, where, when, why, and how, you're probably going to start with *who*. Most likely this will be your organization. Right away you're writing from your interest not your readers'.

For example, a news article introducing new software for a Northern Telecom telephone system began:

Northern Announces New Phone System

Northern Telecom is currently offering a professional time tracking package for the Meridian Norstar Key Telephone System. The time management software is designed for attorneys, architects and advertising agencies. Professionals who bill their time can productively manage and record their client activities—right from their office phone.

This first paragraph includes who, when, what, why and how. The article ends with a detailed list of features. But, it would be better to use the news format as a guideline only. Then, reword it to make it more appealing. For example, in a new product introduction, first tell for whom the product was designed and why it is used. Try to use a catchy lead to do this. Think of your customers. Using this format, the previous example could read as follows:

Money in the Bank as Close as Your Phone

Professionals guard their time like banks guard their vaults. Successful consultants, attorneys, architects and advertising agencies know that productive use of time is money in the bank.

Northern Telecom knows it, too. That's why the time tracking package for the Meridian Norstar Key Telephone System is being offered to professional customers. Using time management software, people who bill their time can productively manage and record their client activities—right from their office phone.

Along with the facts, story telling is important even in news articles. You can add a human element to the strictest of news formats by quoting someone such as your president or a user of the product. The example above could include a quote from an attorney who's tried the product. "The first month I used the system, I billed 10 additional hours that I would have forgotten. The software more than paid for itself right then."

Quotes are also important to report on industry trends. One organization discovered this in the third year of producing its newsletter. The biggest response it had ever received was from an article which was comprised of interviews about an industry trend. The article contained no *new* ideas, just the thoughts on everyone's mind at the time. Interviewing different sources for your articles allows you to "report" on a general consensus.

Show Your Products & Services in Action With a Feature

Once new products and services have been announced, they lose their "newsworthiness." Feature articles allow you to reiterate your product and services by having other people talk about you. Features include articles on clients, case histories, employees and educational information. This can include news of everyday (or unusual) applications or uses of your products.

The style of features encourages promotional writing. The purpose of features is to capture and hold the reader's attention. In well-written features, there is an initial point of contact which is sharp, quick and obvious. A light opening follows to grab the reader's interest. This could be an incident, an anecdote or a conversation. Finally the bulk of the story includes a description and facts. The last paragraph usually concludes the article by repeating the theme. This style is opposite of the news format inverted pyramid style in which the facts are presented first and there is no need for a summary.

When you write features, think of a strawberry packer. Tell the story with sustained interest. Place a layer of good berries on the top but save the best berries for readers to see when they turn the basket upside down. Give almost as much importance in choosing your last sentence as your lead. Words such as "in summary," are signals to your reader that you are bored or that the article has gone on too long and you don't know how to stop it. Quotes work well for endings. Find one which has a sense of finality, is funny, or adds a last surprise.

The hardest part of writing a feature is coming up with a theme and writing the conclusion. By remembering the strawberry packer, you'll know to save an interesting tidbit for last. You'll also use that tidbit to develop the theme for the article. Pack up your berries and come on down to the ranch to see how.

Top Berries:

With a name like RBR Computer Ranch, you'd expect to find this dealer in the outskirts of Dallas or Houston or at least somewhere west of the Rockies. Well, venture into the "cement ranch" of New York's Manhattan and you'll find RBR nestled on the 4th floor at Fifth Avenue and 20th Street.

Why "Computer Ranch?" "You have to be different," says Jose Ristorucci, president of RBR. "Look at Egghead Software, you remember their name before you'd remember Alpha Omega Software. We thought of Computer Zoo, but that was already taken."

Bottom Berries:

The technical knowledge and personal approach found at RBR sets them apart from the rest of the herd. "Every customer has a different need," Ristorucci says. "They can come here or we will go to them. Some days we have five or six people in here being trained or looking at software packages."

Ah, life is good down on the ranch.

It's easier to find themes for some articles than others. For an article on a company who uses a computer product to design a flood control system, finding a theme was easy.

Top Berries:

Reliability—Lives Depend On It

Sierra Misco is in the business of telling people that water runs downhill. The trick is to figure out *how much* water and when it's going to get there. When you're talking about the raging waters of China's Yangtze and Yellow Rivers, that's no small trick.

Bottom Berries:

The systems have to be reliable—people's lives depend on the performance of the equipment.

It's important in an ongoing publication to avoid formula writing. For example, you wouldn't want to start every customer feature with a question. Features can be written in unusual ways. Some subjects give you the opportunity to write truly unique pieces. The writer of this feature obviously enjoyed the assignment. She was profiling two members of an advertising association and the arrival of their twins.

Double Exposure

Jim & Kathy. Devault. Double De. Double DeVault. Double DeVault. Photographer & Illustrator/Graphic Designer. Re-spectively.

Sunset Place. Home plus two Studios. His & Hers. Upstairs, Downstairs. Lots of neon. Double Occupancy. Double Time. Double Digits.

Married 16 years. Can you believe it? Children? Ok, ok...we are?

Get ready. It's a Double Bubble. Twins!?! Great? Double Your Pleasure. Double Your Fun.

Oops. Double Trouble. Stay off your feet for about 4 months...Double Clutch...Jim built a drawing table for her bed...Double shift...He cooks. He Cleans. He keeps Sunset Place Sunny.

Christmas in the hospital. Double Fault.

Fun. Careful. Careful...See you every Wednesday, Doc. Double Your Money.

February 2. Double Jeopardy. Blood test? Check in again. We're going for it? Honey, Could you please drop by the hospital? On the Double!

Two hours later, Here they are...Daniel James, weighing in at 5 pounds even. And, Samuel Taylor, 6 pounds, 1.5 ounces. Double Double Dee-Vault.

They're sooooo cute. Look just like their Daddy. Pandemonium.

Pan-dee-mo-nee-um. Check the chart...who ate when, how much and what? Every three hours. Double vision. Simple Delirium.

Is Kathy asleep?...Double Parked on the couch.

Just ask her to spec some type. Go ahead... I Double Dog Dare Ya!

> One newsletter writer used to joke about her standard "Have you ever wondered?" opening. She would catch herself starting every article with, "Have you ever looked into your closet and wondered how fabric companies keep track of all the different designs?" or "Have you ever wondered where all the old movies are kept?" Since she was aware of her habit, she could go back and modify the formula to give each article a fresh opening.

Before you say, "Hey, you said in the beginning that I didn't have to be a master writer," look and see how this article was written. The main theme is twins, two or double. Open up a dictionary of American idioms and look under *double*. There you'll find: double back, double check, double date, double duty, double-header, double-park, double play, double reverse, double-talk and double up. See? The writer even missed a few that you could work in.

Writing Lively Editorials

Often, you may interview a member of your organization and write the editorial for them. Your job is to encourage them to talk openly to you and not in the way they think an editorial should sound. Spend 30 minutes talking to the person. Then, take his or her opinions and thoughts and write them in an editorial format. You'll save the person lots of time and you'll get the editorial you need, written in the way you want.

Editorials are used to promote your image. They establish the people in your organization as experts. Editorials include letters from the president or an opinion on an industry trend. They are usually written in first person and share ideas, opinions and forecasts.

Before you start to yawn, remember that editorials don't have to be boring. One company president adamantly believed layoffs could be avoided and wanted to share his ideas with readers. His editorial on avoiding layoffs began:

> It was the hardest thing I've ever done. When I looked around at the faces of the nine people I had just called into the conference room, I felt a sharp pain in the pit of my stomach. My voice quavered as I tried to explain why I had to lay them off, but it didn't matter. After my first few strained words, they stopped listening. As far as they were concerned, it was over.

I'm willing to bet you're not yawning nor will your readers be if you choose writers who are evangelists on specific issues and willing to spend the time necessary to write an interesting editorial.

How to Write Elevating Leads

Regardless of the exact format you choose, the first sentence is the most important one your article. If it doesn't pull your climbers into the second one, their climb has stopped.

The opening line of the article is called the lead. From your collection of facts use the most unique, most important, or most unusual item you have. Is there a colorful word or dramatic story you can work in? For most articles, include your readers or their immediate interests in the lead. Don't make readers have to work to find the subject.

Why is the lead so important? An illustration of a good lead and the answer to the question is explained by the following article from a marketing consultant. The following article from an image newsletter is used to illustrate and convince prospects of the service's expertise.

The Fifteen Second Buzzer

College basketball uses the shot clock. The offensive team has forty-five seconds to take a shot at the basket or face a penalty of turning the ball over to the competition.

In marketing your product or service, a similar clock resides in the minds of prospects. It's the time available for you, the marketer, to attract the prospect's attention and motivate that person to invest more in reviewing your benefits. How much time? It could be as little as 10 to 15 seconds before their mental buzzer sounds, and you lose the prospect.

Can you express your company's advantages to a prospect in 15 seconds? Work with others in your company on your 15-second strategy. The results can point the way to inexpensive adjustments you can make to score higher with new business opportunities.

Keep in mind your 15-second shot clock when writing headlines and leads. Use a benefit lead to attract as many readers as possible to your articles. Benefit leads answer the reader's question, "What's in it for me?"

Eliminate Surprises When Buying a Home

It can pay to peek at your credit report before trying to take out a loan. Knowing what information credit agencies have collected on you and your financial habits can save you time and headaches later.

Cut Air Conditioning Bills 50 Percent

First, look at your landscaping. Next, glance at this month's utility bill. Ouch. Okay, put it back in the drawer.

If you need an extra incentive to complete the landscaping job you've been putting off, pare the job down to planting just three trees. That's right, three trees.

That's all the American Forestry Association says you have to plant to cut your air conditioning bill by 10 to 50 percent. Three carefully planted trees to cut your bill in half. What a deal! Here's what you do...

Even when writing straight news style articles, think of how the news affects your readers. Look at the following examples. The first one is written from the publisher's perspective. The second one is rewritten to include readers during the first few seconds.

House Prepares to Consider Catastrophic Health Care Plan

The House of Representatives will soon consider legislation aimed at protecting the nation's elderly from catastrophic health care costs. There are more than 28 million elderly and three million disabled people in the U.S.

Better:

Protecting the Nation's Elderly From Catastrophic Care Costs

Over 28 million elderly people and three million disabled people could be helped by upcoming legislation considered by the House of Representatives.

Leads can also be used to sift out your best prospects. You may only want calls from people ready to buy a certain product or service. Speak directly to those customers in the lead. Here are some examples.

Retirement! It's a time of life we all look forward to. Bask in the sun, play golf, attack those projects you've always wanted to.

If you're interested in PageMaker for the PC, you can get a hands-on introduction with our new demonstration packet.

If you are paying high federal and state taxes, tax-free mutual funds can offer significant advantages.

Not all newsletter articles are written alike. To keep your newsletter fresh, include a variety of styles. An effective way to talk about your products and services is through a problem/solution format.

Have you ever found yourself at a "gala" event staring at a piece of boiled chicken, a hard potato, and a spoonful of peas, garnished with a parsley sprig or orange slice, while a monotone speaker drones on about corporate objectives, projected growth and the value of hard work?

To avoid this familiar scenario, companies hire event specialist Kathleen Starnes of K.M Starnes & Associates. She handles the planning and implementation of corporate events.

Another way to hook readers is by writing about something odd or unusual. Catch their attention and make them say, "What?" Then they'll continue to read out of curiosity.

More and More Doctors are Getting Mumps

Although not widely publicized, Mumps has been spreading rapidly in the medical computing community. But this Mumps is different than the strain you had as a child. The symptoms are sudden organization of once-chaotic clinical records with money mysteriously left over in the computer budget.

Following the Pace Setter

Once you catch readers by showing you have a subject they're interested in or curious about, then your job is to keep them reading. Maintain the pace and mood you've set in the beginning throughout the article.

Brevity is paramount in newsletter writing. It is both physical and psychological. Newsletters are physically shorter than most publications. The brevity of newsletters leaves readers feeling that they have gained maximum information in a minimum amount of time. Busy people like this pace.

Just because your publication looks like a newsletter doesn't automatically assure you'll achieve this brevity. You have to work at it.

There are several writing methods used to pack an article full of information. First, include as much of the story as possible in the headline and don't repeat it in the first paragraph. Then use a short paragraph to begin the copy. The first paragraph should plunge right into the subject and the leading sentence should start the article off with a punch. Short paragraphs throughout your articles add white space to the page and make it look inviting.

Part of your article's fast pace comes from the sifting you do before writing. Then, after the first draft is completed, go back and tighten up your writing again. Cut extraneous words and shorten sentences. For example, use pronouns and abbreviations as a second reference to nouns. "Personal computer" shortens to "PC," "Wallingford B. Smith" becomes "he" and the "University of California at Irvine" reduces to "UCI," "the university," or "it."

You can also condense sentences by looking for single words to replace phrases—such as "now" in place of "at the present time"—and using punctuation devices like a colon, semicolon or dash. If you have quotes in your articles, check to see if information is repeated or summarized outside the quote. If it is, cut it.

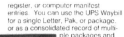

More International Service and Savings

Using The UPS Waybill

The UPS Waybill is an alternate method of recording and labeling international air shipments. It takes the place of pickup record, parcel register, or computer manifest entries. You can use the UPS Waybill for a single Letter, Pak, or package, or as a consolidated record of multiple packages and Paks making up a single shipment.

Two new UPS International Air service offerings depend on the UPS Waybill for documentation. They are: Shipment Pricing savings on multiple package shipments to a single consignee, and collect service — transportation and declared value charges billed to consignee.

The Waybill is a multi-part form that adheres to the package. Your UPS driver will sign in the shaded area (see top left) and separate the copies. One copy stays with you as the shipper's record. One is returned to UPS, and one stays with the package until delivery.

The bottom portion of the Waybill (unseen until the driver separates the copies) contains a package tracking bar code and takes the place of an air tracking label. But, other packages in a multiple-package shipment will each need an air tracking label so they have individual bar code tracking numbers.

Keep Waybill packages separate from other international packages. That's to help your driver spot them. Your UPS driver will make sure the Waybill is filled in, the red air service tracking label is visible, and you get your copy which is your record of shipment with the package tracking number on it.

Your driver can supply you with UPS Waybills. Use the Waybill to expedite international shipping paperwork and to take advantage of Shipment Pricing savings and collect service.

> **UPS Waybill Checklist**
>
> 1. Separate Waybill shipments from other international packages.
>
> 2. Adhere Waybill to only one package in multiple-package shipments. Others in the same shipment each get your standard address label and a red Next Day Air tracking label. All packages get an Export Shipment Control sticker.
>
> 3. Use a Waybill when taking advantage of Shipment Pricing savings for multiple-package shipments to one consignee on one day.
>
> 4. Use a Waybill when specifying collect service (consignee pays transportation and declared value charges).
>
> 5. Remember, use a Waybill only for International Air shipments. The Waybill does not apply to ground service to Canada or service to Puerto Rico.
>
> 6. Keep your copy of the completed UPS Waybill. It is your receipt for the shipment and contains your package tracking number

Your UPS driver signs the Waybill and separates the copies.

UPS Waybill becomes tracking label for the package it is on.

It is often difficult to achieve the feeling of brevity when trying to provide the reader with details. To keep the pace of your article from being bogged down with facts, separate details out of the body of the article and into ruled boxes called sidebars. Specifications, for example, are often important to engineers but not to all readers and can be neatly sectioned off in a sidebar.

Sidebars can also be used to satisfy readers who want their information in a hurry. Consider publishing short "fact boxes" to capsulize vital details of a story in a few paragraphs. Fact boxes and sidebars are placed within or adjacent to the story and visually separated by a box, heavy bars on the top and bottom, or with a screen.

Part of the feeling of brevity is the concentration of information in a short amount of space. If there is not enough information on a topic, either try to find additional sources, or, if possible, hold the story for another issue while information is being collected.

Avoiding Self-Flattery or "Puffery"

Keep in mind that your newsletter is promotional. When appropriate, write sentences from the readers point of view. For example, if you are writing about your recent move to a new facility, you could write "the additional space for assembling and shipping will enable your orders to be packaged and shipped 50 percent faster than before to greatly help your just-in-time delivery needs." Or, less effectively, you could write from your point of view saying, "We are very proud of the new building. It is the manifestation of achieving our sales goals from last year and we couldn't have done it without the help of every employee." This sentence might be inspiring to your employees, but not to your customers.

A good test to make sure your articles are on target is to check for the use of "you" rather than "we." Using "you" not only gets the reader involved, it also gets *you* thinking in terms of the reader. Avoid using "we at..." "We at First Financial are proud to announce that...," sounds stuffy. Instead say, "First Financial now provides you with..."

To effectively speak to your readers, all articles should answer your reader's question: "How does this affect me?"

As with headlines, don't begin every article with your company name. The following opening paragraph from a UPS newsletter borderlines on infringing this rule. It would be better if the first two sentences were reversed.

> On August 28, the company's 82nd anniversary, United Parcel Service announced a vastly expanded list of international destinations. Now you can send both dutiable and non-dutiable shipments to more than 175 countries and territories in the worldwide UPS delivery network.

Much better was the opening sentence in another article from the same newsletter: "UPS Hundredweight Service, introduced earlier this year, is already yielding significant savings to UPS customers."

Once you've written the body of your newsletter article, go back and write the skimmer aides used for image promotion.

Headlines & Subheads That Net in the Skimmers

Realize now that few people read newsletters from cover to cover. Most people will pick it up and "skim." Skimmers read the headlines, subheads, captions and pull quotes, looking to see if they want to take the time to read the article.

Realizing this, your headlines, subheads, pull quotes and captions should contain the bulk of your sales message. They should also entice the reader by summarizing the main ideas, concepts or feelings presented in the article.

Headlines. The headline is the barker for your leading sentence. It captures the readers' attention and delivers them to the lead. Active verbs work well in headlines. So do numbers. The "One Minute Manager" is the title of a book that was remarkably successful. In "Forty Quick Tips to Reduce Your Chances of Cancer," the words "quick" and "tips" are both effective. They tell readers' the book provides fast, condensed information.

Good headlines give your newsletter an edge over competing publications. With research showing more than five times as many people reading headlines as reading the body copy, editors must take the time to write good headlines. Make sure and fill each line to get maximum impact.

All headlines must focus on your readers and tell them the article has some benefit to them. You can use a direct mail trick and offer a benefit in the headline: "17 Ways to Improve Your Business," or "Save 50% by Using New Packaging."

The headline follows the same format as the one you've chosen for your article. It may contain a benefit, an unusual statement or twisted cliche, set up a problem/solution format, or call out to only one segment of your readers. A feature's headline may be a quote from one of the interviewees.

Make sure your headlines aren't victims of puffery. Avoid starting with your company name or product names. An extreme example of this is an eight-page newsletter from a company called Quadram. The headlines for the first four pages were:

> Quadram Enters Communications Market With LANs
> Quadnets Expand IBM PC Communications Abilities
> Quadmodem Opens Communications Channels For Micros
> Quadram Establishes the Micro-Mainframe Connection
> Quadmem Jr. Makes PC JR a Master
> Quadram's Amberchrome Monitor Refreshes IBM PCs
> Quadchrome II Offers Hi Rez Color For IBMs

With every headline beginning with "Quad," the headlines don't stand alone as offering unique benefits to read the articles. They quickly tell climbers, "These articles are written from our point of view." That's not the message you want to convey in your promotional newsletter.

Subheads. After you write the headline, look at the other promotional points in your article and use them as subheads. Subheads are used to divide lengthy articles into logical breaks. They may indicate to the reader a change of topic, a link of content, or simply break up a mass of type. Subheads placed about every four paragraphs also allow readers to skip sections of the article without losing their train of thought. By including subheads, you'll also retain skimmers. Subheads are generally viewed as a goodwill gesture. They say, "I've made an extra effort to communicate."

Most importantly, subheads include your top promotional points. Look at the following article. By skimming the title, lead, subheads and conclusion, you read the main sales points of the article in a few seconds. Your shot is off before the buzzer!

	Lightning Never Strikes Twice
Deck	But if it does, Enco knows Dalcon will be there.
Lead	On Monday morning, June 27, systems operator Monica Ball arrived to work and was greeted by the smell of smoke.
Subhead	Calling on Dalcon
Subhead	Up and running by noon
Subhead	Sharing the burden
Conclusion	"I know that when I call Dalcon, it will no longer be *my* problem. It will be *our* problem."

Captions (also called Cutlines). Captions are the descriptive text placed under, over, or to the side of a photo. Pay special attention to your captions. Along with the headlines, this is one of the first places readers look. Include your primary promotional message here. Also, include information that draws people into the article. Most people read the caption first to see if they want to read the accompanying article.

	Child Sponsorship: Saving Families From Ruin
Lead	Life in Potosi, Bolivia, and its suburbs is hard. Unemployment is high, and poverty has taken control.
	Thanks to you, however, two families are on the road to a better future.
Caption	Education is paving the way for the future of the Castro Quispe family in Bolivia. Thank you for caring.
Caption	The Marco Soto family is being fed both physically and spiritually, thanks to your precious donations in Bolivia.

Atlantis Pools & Spas offers both pre-designed pools and spas as well as unique designs for you and your yard. The pool above was designed and installed by Atlantis' Leo Shapiro. He used Arkansas stone for the deck, walk-up steps, and waterfall.

While a photograph can capture the attention of your reader, the caption sells your idea. A pool installation company shows one of its pool designs in each issue. Every photograph includes a caption describing the design along with its features and benefits.

Decks. Instead of repeating part of the main article, you may want to begin the article with an attention getting statement. These follow the headline and are called decks. A deck is a few lines of description placed *underneath* the headline. It can be used to give the reader more information about the article without using a gigantic headline. An effective deck guides readers into the rest of the article before they know it.

Titanic Explorers' Problem Solved by Black Box

Deck   April 15, 1912.

The "unsinkable luxury ocean liner, the *Titanic*, collides with an iceberg and sinks, carrying 1,552 passengers and crew to the bottom of the sea. Along with the first-class passengers, who had paid the equivalent of $50,000 for the trip, go millions of dollars in cash, jewelry, artifacts and art.

It's the stuff of legend.

And legend it remained, until 1985, when the Woods Hole Oceanographic Institution discovered the location of the wreck.

A year later, using an underwater robot, the same group was able to explore and film inside the Titanic.

The body of the article tells how a Black Box product helped the robot.

Kickers. A kicker is a line run in smaller type *above* the headline. It helps keep the headline shorter. A kicker is often used for regular features such as editorials, technical support tips, newsbriefs or updates. Kickers give the writer the freedom to write a new headline for each article rather than using the kicker as the title every time.

The president of a computer dealership wrote an article for each of the company's newsletters. Every issue, he would choose a subject he thought was of interest to other business owners. Here is his kicker and some of the headlines.

Kicker   **OWNER TO OWNER:**

Headline   **Newsletters: We All Know the Worth, But Oh the Struggle!**

Kicker   **OWNER TO OWNER:**

Headline   **How Do We Get the Numbers We Need?**

Pull Quotes (also called Callouts, Lift-out Quotes or Outquotes). Pull quotes are commonly used by magazines and newsletters to draw readers into long articles. A pull quote is a sentence taken from an article and enlarged to catch reader interest. They are also used as a layout device to break up type and add white space.

Choose sentences or phrases which stand alone, are interesting or shout out one of your promotional points. Make sure pull quotes retain their meaning when read out of context.

> *"Do you want to trust the safety of your friends and family to a brake part that is a dollar cheaper?"*

This is a pull quote from an auto parts manufacturer's newsletter. The article compared name-brand to off-brand components. The pull quote contains the main promotional point of the article.

Inspiring Readers to Open Your Newsletter

Once all of your articles are written, return to the subjects and motivating words you chose to promote specifics. Use these words for the teasers and contents box that readers see first when looking at the newsletter. The box should encourage readers to open the publication. You can use teasers to attract attention or to capture the readers you desire. If you want tax clients, write "Important Tax Information Enclosed." If you're promoting to retailers, exclaim "Important News For Retailers." Of course, make sure you have covered these subjects inside.

Describe your feature articles by telling readers the benefits of reading them. The contents box at the right could be used on the mailing panel as a teaser to attract your attention.

INSIDE:

- How to get your newsletter out on time
- Production tips for improving your newsletter
- Convert newsletter information into on-hold advertising

Your contents box may just include the titles of your newsletter articles. This makes it easier for readers to find the articles they want. However, if your newsletter is under eight pages, either use a contents box as a teaser on the mailing panel or eliminate it and use the space for something else.

Now you know how to guide your readers through your newsletter using words. You can pack extra information into your articles and attract even more readers by using graphics such as photographs, charts, cartoons and illustrations. These are covered in the next chapter.

11

Designing Road Signs For Readers

Your newsletter is comprised of several different design elements. These are the road signs used to direct readers through the publication. Design elements can make readers stop, take a detour, or move through the newsletter in a certain direction. Most design road signs are produced once. They are posted either in every issue or only when needed. For example, the nameplate appears on every newsletter. On the other hand, sidebars and photographs are included only when available or needed.

Most road signs have a straightforward, clean, professional appearance. This gives the impression that the newsletter is produced by the kind of organization you'd like to belong to or do business with. Through illustrations, photographs of people, and color, you can convey a friendly, approachable image that warms up prospects and supporters.

This chapter shows you how to design each promotional newsletter road sign to achieve your desired goals.

Road Signs for Recognition

Readers move through the recognition level at top speed. Graphics are important for quickly prompting reader recognition and interest. Because most readers see your newsletter as they sort the day's stack of mail, you must make your newsletter pop out, and draw your reader into the publication immediately. Readership declines if the newsletter isn't opened right away.

The design elements important to recognition are size, the mailing panel, the contents box and teasers, and the nameplate.

Size—Standing Out in the Mail Stack

Does your newsletter get stacked in with the magazines, fliers, letters or somewhere in between? Your newsletter's page size and number of folds determines where it lands in the stack.

The standard page size of most newsletters is 8½" x 11" inches. Standard sizes have the advantages of cost, matching standard envelopes, and fitting in binders if readers want to save them (and many do).

If you mail a standard size newsletter flat, it falls with the magazines. If you fold it down to 5½" x 8½", it's between the magazines and the letters. And, if you fold it like a letter and mail it with or without an envelope, it appears with the letters. Because magazines are set aside for later reading, stay out of the magazine area by folding your newsletter for mailing.

The most attention-getting location of the mail stack is on top with the letters. People pay special attention to this section. They look here for personalized correspondence and checks. If your newsletter is more than four pages, however, it may be too thick when folded in three.

Instead, you may choose to fold the newsletter in half for mailing. Many promotional newsletters are mailed this way. If your readers enjoy newsletters and look for them in their stack, your newsletter may get picked out of the bunch. By folding the newsletter in half versus in thirds, you have more room on the mailing panel for teasers and other information about the content of the newsletter.

Newsletters are sometimes mailed in envelopes. Some promotional newsletter publishers feel it's well worth the expense. Newsletters mailed in envelopes arrive in better condition and look more like official correspondence. Envelopes also allow you to cover the entire newsletter with editorial content since a mailing panel is unnecessary. Other fliers and reply cards can be added to the package without inserting them in the publication.

To stand apart, some organizations print oversized (9" x 12" for example) newsletters. Others—those with lots of news—expand to a tabloid (11" x 17") or a newsprint (11" x 15") size. These page sizes also provide more space to enlarge photographs, enhancing the piece's visual appeal.

Over-sized pieces also cost more to mail. If your newsletter is sent to designers or other types of people who place great value on the unusual, consider an oversized newsletter. Otherwise, save your printing and mailing budget.

Mailing Areas That Say "Read Me"

Once your newsletter makes it out of the mail stack, the reader glances at the return address and mailing area. This is a strategic moment. If the reader recognizes your name or the publication and remembers it as being of value, it gets opened. Otherwise, you must convince readers to take the next step.

Use the mailing area of your newsletter for more than just a label. For the first few issues of your newsletter, while the publication is establishing recognition, give the mailing area of your newsletter special attention. If you continue to add new readers or buy different mailing lists, continue to give this area top priority.

If they don't recognize the piece, most readers look first to the return address. To increase recognition, place your organization's logo here. If it's not well known, add a slogan or mission statement so readers know what you do. For some organizations a slogan is not sufficient. They list all of their services and perhaps even a location map. Immediately under this information, place a contents box or a teaser. Tell prospective readers why they should open up the publication right now.

Of course, all of this can't fit on the mailing panel while retaining a simple, professional design. Choose the elements most important for your organization's promotion.

Teasers may be used to tell readers one important piece of information such as a notice of an upcoming meeting or where to find you at a trade show.

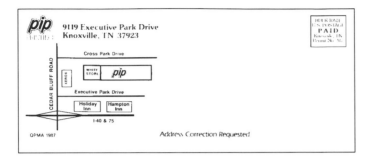

Location maps are important for retailers in highly competitive markets. The convenience of your location can help make the sale. Draw a map or write a few directions. If you offer free pickup and delivery, print this in bold characters instead of the map.

When mailing your newsletter yourself, you may be tempted to staple it shut. Don't. Without a staple remover, it is almost impossible to open the newsletter without ripping it. After all of your hard work, why ruin your promotional punch with a tattered letter?

The post office does not require fastening of loose sheets. If you need to use a closure to hold in inserts, stickers or tape work better and allow the reader to open the piece without ripping it.

Nameplate—The Foundation of Your Newsletter's Design

Once you've gained readers' attention, they open the newsletter. The first graphic element they see is the nameplate. The nameplate of your newsletter is the stylized representation of the newsletter name along with other information. Be forewarned, though, that this is often mistakenly called a "masthead." A masthead is the box of information concerning the publishing, copyright, circulation and other items about the publication.

The nameplate is the cornerstone for the design of your newsletter. It's impossible to have a well-designed newsletter without a good nameplate. But with a good nameplate, the rest of your newsletter can be very plain and the piece still looks professional. Design your own nameplate only if you have a qualified designer on staff. Otherwise, subcontract this one-time, worthwhile expense.

Readers notice and remember unique nameplate designs. The nameplate is the "you are here" sign. It identifies the publication, your organization, and its products, services or purpose. For readers who are unfamiliar with your organization, the nameplate communicates its purpose or market niche. This is achieved through the name and subtitle you choose.

For readers familiar with your organization, one way to prompt recognition is to design your newsletter similar to your other printed pieces. You can use your organization's logo and colors as part of the design. Then your newsletter will complement other publicity such as print advertising, catalogs, direct mail and trade show displays. This gives consistency to all your promotions.

The following promotional nameplates contain the logo of the publisher. Notice how the organizations' logos accent, rather than overpower, the name of the newsletter.

© 1989 United Parcel Serivce of America. Reprinted with permission.

Along with providing repetition of your company name, location and products, your newsletter can reinforce other marketing efforts. Use your logo and other standard design elements in your nameplate if you usually group marketing materials together for press kits or promotional packets.

The nameplates of promotional newsletters are designed to be immediately recognizable as coming from a specific organization. Effective nameplates are simple and contain only a few elements. The largest of the elements is the type containing the name of the publication. Strong bold typography is often enough to create an attractive nameplate.

A computer dealer uses a mountain in its logo in some of its marketing. One of its campaigns emphasizes the importance of choosing a mountain climbing partner you can trust and communicate with. in the newsletter nameplate a mountain, along with the word "summit," reinforces this ongoing campaign.

Sometimes a graphic or photograph is added as an accent to the nameplate. Like logos, graphics should never overpower the type containing the name of the newsletter.

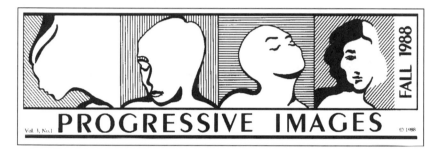

Along with identifying the publication and the publisher, the nameplate can be used to communicate your publication schedule. This is done by the way you list the date. Date a monthly "January," a bi-monthly "January/February," and a quarterly "1st Quarter" or according to the four seasons.

Some newsletters follow a system used by subscription publications and print volumes and numbers along with the date. Volumes and numbers are used primarily by libraries to aid in cataloging publications. They can also indicate to your readers the length of time your publication has been produced. For example, "Volume 3 Number 4" indicates the third year of publishing and the fourth newsletter of that particular year. Use them only if stability and longevity are important to your prospects. If so, add them after your first year of publishing. Since space is a premium on most nameplate designs, consider putting the volume and number in the masthead.

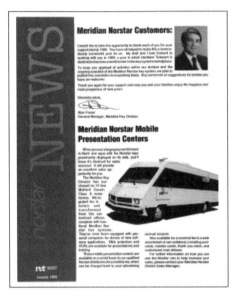

Vertical placement of the nameplate can create an attractive design. But make sure the nameplate doesn't interfere with the front page articles.

As far as its relation to the design of your newsletter as a whole, the nameplate is usually placed horizontally at the top of the first page. Some organizations, however, place it vertically.

Once the readers get past the nameplate to the first article in the newsletter, other design elements start to work. These elements guide readers through the rest of the newsletter.

Image: Quick communication continues

Remember the shot clock from the last chapter? The 15 to 20 seconds you have to attract your reader is the total amount of time you have for both recognition and image. The graphic tools used for recognition are designed to encourage your prospect to open the publication. Graphics inspire readers to start skimming.

Several design elements work together to draw the reader. The paper determines how the graphics, extra color, and type appear on the page. Color highlights important items by drawing readers' eyes to titles or a two-line message. Graphics and photographs also capture your reader's eye. Obviously, everything on your newsletter page can't be fighting for attention. When you combine road signs to form the layout, highlight only the most important promotional items.

Paper—The Right Touch

From crisp reproduction of photographs to conveying ecological concerns, paper sets the image of your newsletter. The weight, texture and finish of your newsletter's paper determine how it feels in readers' hands. Because heavy paper gives a solid, stable image, most organizations print on paper weights of 70# text and higher. Aside from its stable image, thicker paper also eliminates bleedthrough of printing on the reverse side.

An added texture, such as a linen finish, can also boost the "thickness" of the paper. One of the main drawbacks to using textured paper, however, is that photographs don't reproduce as well as they do when printed on a smooth surface.

For economic reasons, uncoated papers with a vellum, or smooth, finish are commonly used for newsletters. Uncoated papers are resilient for mailing and work well for newsletters without photographs. If you regularly include photographs, investigate using coated paper. There are three kinds of coated papers used for publications: gloss, matte coated, or dull coat.

On glossy paper, photographs appear crisper and colors brighter than on uncoated paper. But it is also the type of paper used for most brochures. A newsletter that looks too slick may have the psychological drawback of appearing like a sales promotion rather than useful news. Depending on the lighting in your reader's office or home, glossy paper can be hard to read because of light reflection.

A possible compromise is matte finished paper—a coated sheet but without a glossy finish. Matte finished paper reproduces photographs and colors well and diffuses light better. Dull coat also reproduces extremely well, but can be more expensive than a matte coated stock.

If you want to give your readers the feeling of receiving late breaking news, you may consider printing on newsprint. Although the paper is thin, it tends to hold the ink well and it can be jazzed up with an extra color.

One last thought on paper. Many readers are sensitive to the need to recycle paper. You can show your support by printing on recycled paper. Both coated and uncoated grades are available. If you choose a recycled paper, inform readers. Print the recycle logo and the line "This newsletter is printed on recycled paper" somewhere in the newsletter.

For readers wanting to recycle your newsletter, uncoated paper and newsprint are recyclable. At this time, coated paper is not. Many environment-oriented groups have been blasted by members when they've printed promotional materials on coated paper.

Off With Flying Colors

Colors set the mood of your publication—from friendly to formal. Colors are also important for attracting readers.

It has been estimated that readership increases threefold if a publication is illustrated with a second ink color. But to preserve legibility, use color judiciously. For example, print your text in black ink on white paper. Then, to attract the reader's eye, use a second ink color, known as "spot color," for headlines, bars, captions and other elements of the layout.

To keep the design of marketing pieces consistent, use your organization's color as the spot color. Your main color may be dark enough to print text and you can choose a second color for highlight. Some editors change the second color of the newsletter from issue to issue. This helps readers recognize each issue as a new one, rather than each issue looking the same at first glance. You may even have the printing budget for three colors.

There are several rules of thumb for choosing legible ink and paper colors. For best legibility, keep the color of the paper as light as possible and the color of the ink as dark as possible. Black ink on white paper is always the easiest on the eyes. Dark blue, dark green, brown or charcoal ink are nearly as legible.

Another method of making the newsletter colorful is by printing on colored paper. Most designers, though, recommend using white paper with two ink colors instead.

Colors arouse emotion. Colors of stability are dark blue and dark green. A publication printed with black ink and dark green or dark blue as highlight colors looks very formal. If you're promoting a bank or an investment firm, this may be important to your image. Gray also gives a dignified image and is pleasing to the eye, but can be depressing. With this in mind, avoid printing on gray paper. Keep in mind that the darker the color of ink, the less it attracts the eyes of readers. If you have some design leeway, use bright colors.

Brighter colors are more friendly—bright blue, teal, purple or melon. The most attention-grabbing colors are red, orange and yellow. But if you want to suggest stability, avoid

An event planner changed the colors of the confetti and headlines on each issue to create the mood for the coming holidays. Her Christmas issue was red, spring was purple, summer was yellow, and fall was orange. The color creates a festive appeal and tells prospects the events she produces are full of pizzazz.

bright red. Bright red should also be avoided by hospitals and other health professionals because of its association with blood. The same goes for banks, accountants and financial institutions. Customers want to be "in the black," not "in the red." Burgundy is a suitable substitute for bright red.

Since research has shown that people retain a message longer if it's printed in black and white, use your second color for highlight only and print text in a dark color. Or, highlight the text area by framing in the entire page with the second color.

Even if your budget only allows for one ink color, create more colors from it by using screens.

Creating Other Colors. Screens give one- and two-color publications the effect of having many colors. A screen creates the illusion of another color by breaking the color into dots. Each dot is 100 percent of the ink color.

Screens are used to highlight or separate areas of your newsletter such as a short article, sidebars, contents boxes and tables. Some ink colors when screened create a highlight that draws your eye to that area. Yellow, orange, purple, and other bright colors create eye-attracting screens. Some screened colors help separate blocks of text.

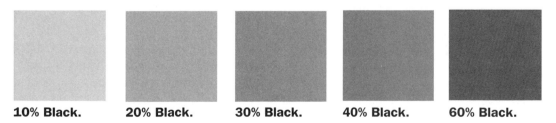

10% Black.   **20% Black.**   **30% Black.**   **40% Black.**   **60% Black.**

Many desktop publishing programs now allow you to combine colors and visualize the effect quickly on a color monitor. If you're printing with black and bright blue, for example, you can combine the two colors in a screened box and create dark blue. If your organization's color is dark blue, you may be able to mix black and bright blue to make the color and use it for your logo and maybe in the nameplate. Then you can use the bright blue as a highlight color.

Shells. One way to save money when printing more than one color is to pre-print a large quantity of shells. Shells are pages of your newsletter pre-printed with colors you won't be using for text. If you want to use shells, design the publication so that the second color areas are in fixed places from issue to issue. Preprint the second color onto your newsletter's paper. Your printer stores the pre-printed paper for you. Then, for each issue, the printer adds the text and photos in the main color, usually black.

For promotional newsletters, shells have some serious drawbacks. Pre-printed shells may keep you from using color to draw attention to a special promotional item. For most promotional newsletters this is too inflexible. Instead, find a printer who frequently runs the highlight color you've chosen—maybe the printing company has a large client using a similar color. Or, perhaps you can strike a deal to get the second color free if you print on a certain day. Many quick printers have days when certain second colors are free.

Using shells is also not advisable for rapidly-changing organizations or for the first few issues of your newsletter. You're bound to want to make changes. If you can design your publication with promotional highlights in fixed places, print up some shells. Otherwise, look at other ways to save money.

Color is one of the best tools you have for attracting the reader's eye. Use it strategically and judiciously.

Draw in Readers With White Space

Color is more than spot color. The paper you print on and the dark ink you use for body copy can also create colors—from white space with no text, to the "gray" formed by words on a page.

Think of the warm feeling you get when someone invites you to a party. People like to be included and made comfortable. Add some Southern hospitality to your newsletter. Beckon readers to your publication by defining points of entry with white space, headlines, kickers and initial caps.

Headlines, kickers and initial caps signal readers where to start. The more articles you have on a page, the more points of entry you've created.

Just as walking into a crowded room of strangers is intimidating, so is a page filled only with text. Many publishers are tempted to cram every last bit of news onto a page. After all, blank space is a lost opportunity to promote. While this is true, extra white space can actually help hold the reader's attention.

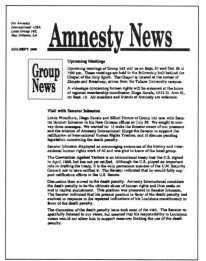

White space is created by page margins, subheads, pull quotes, headlines and captions. These elements break up what would otherwise be a mass of "gray." Large blocks of type are called "blocks of gray" because that's the way the page looks if you hold it at a distance.

Leaving extra white space at the top of pages gives visual relief from large blocks of gray. It helps the reader move more quickly through the publication. Subheads and pull quotes are also used in long articles. They separate columns of text into smaller, less intimidating blocks.

By using a scholar's margin and subheads, this text-only newsletter looks more inviting.

Photographs Provide Instant Communication

The best way to break up blocks of type on a page is by using graphics such as photographs, illustrations, charts and cartoons. Statistics show that about twice as many people read articles that are illustrated. Carefully choose graphics that enforce and enhance your promotional message. Remember, readers retain visual images longer than they retain words.

Photographs play an important role in providing condensed information. Rather than taking several sentences to describe a product or person, a photo can be used. Photographs of people also provide an element of emotion by showing smiling, concentrating or concerned faces.

If you're using several presentation pictures showing recipients of awards, photograph the group together with their plaques after the ceremony. This avoids the dreaded "yearbook" effect of having rows of photographs in your newsletter. It also avoids having your executives appear in the photos as often as your clients or members—they're not the ones being recognized.

Photo: Dennis Carney.

Many people are afraid of computers and other equipment. If you show a photograph of the equipment, prospects may be intimidated rather than inspired to call you. Use a photograph to help ease their fears. Show people and results rather than the equipment. Show people interacting with your products in a happy, human way.

The quality of photographs can greatly affect the overall quality of your publication. Even though you may not be in the position to hire a professional to take each picture, remember that using in-focus, candid, interesting photographs improves the look of each page.

Try using unusual angles if you are photographing a common object. Anyone who reads computer magazines is bored with shots of PCs. The photographer of the picture to the left, however, just varied the usual angle and took a great shot.

The following are some resources for professional-quality photographs.

Keeping Photo Files. For an on-going publication, save all of the photographs you receive on file. Photographs you've already used may be run again in a follow up article. Once run, it's a good idea to file photos by issue for easy retrieval. Those not chosen for a particular issue may be needed for a different article.

Make your photographs and headlines match when possible. This clearly communicates to readers the subject of the article. A lot of promotion—perhaps enough to win a customer—can be achieved in these two areas. Often, readers aren't interested in the subject at the time they receive the newsletter. If your message is retained, though, they can return to the article when the need arises.

If you are going to highlight employees or members or have internally-written columns, pictures should accompany the article. Save time and increase quality by having everyone's picture taken at once.

When including photographs of employees, make sure they look friendly and approachable. If your first attempt results in an unflattering or unfriendly photograph, publish the article without it and try again.

From the Sales Team
by
Julia Bailin & Tammy Macdonald

Give the photograph as much "texture" as possible. A wool jacket looks more friendly than slick pin stripe; a sweater more approachable than a suit and tie.

Assuming you're going to run black and white pictures versus color, take the photographs using black and white film. Take several candid shots of each person and choose the most appealing one.

Sources of good photographs. Sometimes you may not have the luxury of taking photographs yourself. If you're reporting on someone else's products or people and they're hundreds of miles away, call their public relations or advertising department and find out if a photograph is available.

If you regularly ask your subjects to take photographs themselves, design a photograph requirements list. Include specifications for black and white or color photographs. Request that your product appear in the picture along with your customer.

Hiring a professional can ensure you get top quality photographs. Check references and follow the procedure for hiring vendors listed in Appendix A. For out of town shots, find a photographer in that area to take the picture for you.

You can rent photographs of common sites like the Grand Canyon or the Moon. These are called stock photographs. The fee you pay is for a one-time use. Several stock photograph services are listed in Appendix B.

When Not to Show Photographs. Many smaller organizations choose not to show pictures of their building or group pictures of their departments. These publishers are maximizing one of the major benefits of newsletters—positioning an organization as a leader and industry expert. Because many people

> A manufacturer reprinted an entire issue of a newsletter that contained a picture of one of the company's divisions. Because he was promoting to large corporations, the president felt that the photo made his company look too small. He felt so strongly about the cost of this perception that he was willing to reprint the entire job.

Both a pie chart and a bar graph accompany this article to explain the type of products computer dealers are selling.

associate leadership and expertise with size, you may not want to draw attention to size if your organization is small.

Sum Up the Numbers With Charts & Graphs

Charts, graphs and diagrams are used when numbers and statistical data are important to your promotions. Use them to represent numbers in a quickly-digestible form. Your organization may want to show how your products are used, what type of members you have, or how donations are appropriated. Instead of listing the percentages or numbers of each, construct a pie chart or bar graph.

Similar to the use of sidebars, charts and diagrams keep your article from getting bogged down with numerical data. People would rather look at a graph of sales or production data than read the numbers. Graphic methods also help readers remember the information.

You don't have to be a graphic artist to create a unique and successful graphic. The trick is to keep it as simple as possible. For example, donations can be shown in a bar graph with the bars made from canned goods or stacks of coins. Add a caption underneath your charts and graphs to tell readers data's significance.

Cartoons Show the Lighter Side

People like to laugh. Salespeople frequently tell their prospects funny stories and jokes. Laughter is an important part of making your prospects look forward to your visits. Regularly including cartoons has the same effect for your newsletter. Even if readers are opening it only to look at the cartoon, you've elevated them to the image level.

People used to think that cartoons destroyed an organization's image or dignity. However, this trend is reversing. It is now recognized that cartoons lend an approachable image to an organization.

Cartoons included in your newsletter offer several benefits. They help explain abstract ideas, draw attention to a related article, and add a human element. Unlike photographs, they have the power to exaggerate the truth while making it real and understandable.

Cartoons in promotional publications highlight the humor in your special area. Check the appendix for clip art and cartoon services. Or, look in your industry magazines for cartoons appropriate for your newsletter. Write for permission to reprint them. Most cartoonists charge a nominal fee.

To avoid seeking reprint permission, convert your own ideas by contracting a cartoonist or artist. Decide the most important promotional point of an article and have a cartoon drawn to emphasize it—speedy delivery, quality control, friendly service.

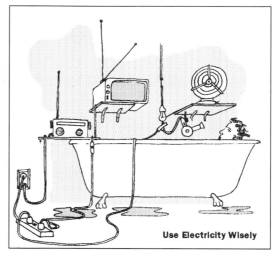

Use Electricity Wisely

Though few readers will finish a long article on electrical safety, everyone will pause to look at this cartoon from an electric service, which gives exactly the same message.

If possible, use the same cartoonist or illustration artist throughout your newsletter. When cartoons are frequently used, they become an important part of your newsletter's design.

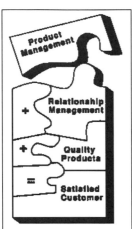

A bank used a graphic to show readers how its customer service department was organized and how the different departments functioned together.

Getting Personal
Different ideas and methods for utilizing personalization in mailers.

You can use graphics along with the kickers for standard features. Readers will become accustomed to looking for the graphic that covers their interest.

Clip Art & Custom Illustrations

Custom illustrations and clip art are used similarly to cartoons. They can emphasize the main point of your article. Often, illustrations are used when you can't find a photograph to accompany the article. Even when a photograph is available, custom drawings or clip art may more accurately communicate your promotional point.

For many associations and non-profit organizations, up-to-date calendars are an important part of their newsletters. You can find clip art and calendars in an art supply store.

Clip art can be purchased on sheets, in collections, in books, or on electronic disks and is usually organized by subject. Quality varies from one supplier to another. Before buying large collections, get samples of the work and make sure it's in the public domain (not protected by copyright). Some clip art is limited to use in a publication of non-commercial purposes. Read the copyright provisions of any collection you buy.

Make Reading a Breeze

Encourage prospects to read your message by making reading easy. The less work readers' eyes have to do, the more energy readers have to think about your messages.

Ease the burden of reading by choosing a common typeface. Certain typefaces are "known" to our brains, such as those used in newspapers. Since most people read word by word—not letter by letter—it's important to have words in your newsletter look the way people are used to reading them. Some typefaces are more formal than others. You can use the typeface to create a mood in your newsletter. It can be formal or informal. The typography can also communicate a feeling of being a direct communication, like a letter.

In addition to the typography, choosing the number and width of columns for each page influences the ease of reading. Column width determines the number of words on each line. It also determines how much work readers have to do.

Type—Increase Your Readers' Endurance

When selecting the typography for your newsletter, you may be choosing from hundreds of faces available from a typesetter, or you may be choosing from those you have on your desktop publishing system. Before we get into the specific choices, keep in mind your primary goal is to make the newsletter easy to read.

The most common point sizes for newsletters are 9, 10 and 11. Use 11 point for the quickest scanning and easiest reading.

The typography, unlike other design elements, should not be immediately noticed by the reader. If it is, you've chosen typefaces that readers have never seen before. Since readers aren't used to recognizing words in an unfamiliar style, their brains must work harder to comprehend what you've written.

The benefit of having a basic desktop publishing system is that you probably have some forms of the most common typefaces like Times Roman and Helvetica. (These are typefaces or type families, not "fonts" as they are mistakenly called in many computer programs.) Most readers can easily distinguish words in these typefaces. They may have trouble, however, if you set large chunks of body copy in bold, italic or all capital letters. Any of these styles will make the body copy harder to read.

Be forewarned that some designers emphasize design over ease of reading. It's your job to look out for your reader. To assure easy reading, have the designer originally set several paragraphs in the chosen style. Test for easy reading before you approve the type.

Ah, those nasty little dates in the corners of our newsletters. They usually mean only one thing– deadlines. But the beauty of these dates is that they show that you always get another chance to make it better. Part of "making the next one better" is trying new ideas. This doesn't mean that you use the front page to try a new color combination or story idea. Experiment with the less noticeable pages first.	Ah, those nasty little dates in the corners of our newsletters. They usually mean only one thing–deadlines. But the beauty of these dates is that they signify the fact that you always get another chance to make it better. Part of "making the next one better" is trying new ideas. This doesn't mean that you use the front page to try a new color combination or story idea. Experiment with the less noticeable pages first.

The first text is set in Lubalin Graph. This typeface is designed to be a display face and used for headlines and larger text. From a distance, it looks more flashy. But readers' eyes have to work much harder than in the second example, set in Caslon.

If your designer suggests a typeface you think is hard to read, choose some others and show them to the artist or test them on potential readers. To find good examples of typefaces, look in magazines and newspapers. Consider a more unusual style for headlines.

An alternative to choosing professionally-set typography is to compose your newsletter using a letter-quality printer or a typewriter. Some people feel that newsletters produced on a typewriter are more personal and have the image of containing the "inside scoop." Many subscription newsletters, such as *The Kiplinger Washington Letter*, are produced this way and *do* contain the inside scoop.

Typed newsletters also carry the image of being a personalized letter. If you are a consultant—a one-person law practice, a financial planner, an accountant—consider this format. It gives prospects the impression of having a one-on-one talk with you. This way you are a "person" and not an "organization." Even for larger firms, a letter to clients carries the image of being an additional service rather than a promotion.

Consider a typed letter also if you're trying to stretch your newsletter budget. With typeset composition, however, you can pack as much as 50 percent more content into the available space. For a lengthy, widely distributed publication, the savings on printing and first class postage can pay for the typesetting alone.

One-column format.

Number of Columns Determines Reading Pace

Another design element affecting the readability of the type is the number of columns. Column width, like typography, can greatly affect your prospect's reading endurance. The proper column width along with the right size and style of type can promote fast, easy reading. This increases comprehension by decreasing eye fatigue.

The number of columns in most newsletters varies from one to four. Advantages and disadvantages exist for both. For most newsletters, a line length of 35 to 45 characters has been found to be the most comfortable to the eye. Most readers have difficulty when reading extremely long or short lines.

The longest lines appear in the one-column format. This format preserves the feel of a "letter" and is the way many typed newsletters look.

Finding ways to reduce line length can increase readability when using the one-column format. One of the best ways is to have a deep left margin called a "scholar's margin." Placing or extending headlines, subheads, sketches and photographs into the scholar's margin decreases the line length and improves readability. Readers can also use the margin for notes or comments.

For larger type sizes, newsletters with two equal columns provide a comfortable line length. A two-column format, however, is rigid from a design viewpoint. Each page is split in half making it difficult to create pages with visual appeal. Visual appeal is often caused by imbalance rather than the perfect balance found in two-column formats. A more flexible format is three columns.

One-column format with scholar's margin.

The three-column format gives the feel of a newspaper or magazine and has become the most common design for newsletters. The popularity of a three-column format is due to the flexibility it provides for the layout, while keeping

Two-column format.

Three-column format.

Four-column format.

the average number of words per line at a level that's easy to read. Photographs, text and headlines can be placed in one of the three columns, or stretched across two.

A four-column format also provides flexibility for illustrations and headlines. For newsletters which have short stories and several photographs, using four columns causes your articles to take up more depth than using three columns. The shorter line lengths, however, can disturb the reader's eye rhythms. The line length is even more awkward if you use excessively long words.

Along with your choice of columns, you must also decide between justified and ragged right formats.

The decision to use ragged right over justified text is usually based on desired image and personal taste. It has no effect on ease of reading. In *Typography: How to make it most legible*, Rolf F. Rehe cites three independent tests proving no difference in readability between justified text and ragged right.

Most designers agree that justified text has a more formal look than ragged right. Make your choice based on the image you'd like to portray. If using a four-column format, however, use ragged right. Because of the shorter line length, spacing between words is awkward when columns are justified.

End of the Line

If your newsletter contains long articles and some of them are continued onto other pages, use an end mark to show readers the end of each article.

End marks are special small graphics such as a symbol, a square, or an element from your nameplate or organization's logo. They provide an extra graphic touch while also avoiding confusion as readers move through the newsletter.

If you are interested in donating items to Goodwill or know of others who are, please make use of the Attended Collection Centers (listed on the back page) or call 742-4161 to arrange a home pick-up. 🔲

In *The Goodwill Ambassador*, the organization's logo is used as an end mark for the articles.

Readers must work hard to receive your promotional messages written in articles. It's much easier for them to peruse the mailing panel, headlines, subheads and other "skimmable" spots. Through typography, you can increase your readers' endurance. With the energy they have left, they just might give you the response you want.

Encourage Saving & Sharing

Without using a lot of words, you can often tell readers what you want them to do after reading your newsletter. You can tell them to save the publication, pass it along to a co-worker, return the reply card, or call you. These traffic signals help you win a response.

To encourage readers to save the newsletter as a reference, punch or "drill" three holes in the binding. This is appropriate for any newsletter, especially technical supplements. Most users of your products and services save technical information, knowing they may need it for future reference. Rather than pre-punching, some publishers provide preprinted circles or extra room along the left margin of the front to prompt three-hole punching.

Along with adding holes, encourage your readers to save the publication by distributing binders. Offer the binder as an incentive for completing a readership questionnaire. Or, print a coupon for it in your newsletter to gauge (and encourage) readership. When designing the binder, make sure your organization's name is printed along the spine. This displays it in front of your reader's eyes when stored on a shelf.

If you are promoting to large organizations, keep in mind that people share information. Often, you may not be able to find everyone within an organization that influences the use or purchase of your services. Especially if you promote to large organizations, add a routing box to your newsletter (see page 98).

Once your newsletter is passed along, the new readers may want to be permanently added to your mailing list. Provide them with the information to contact you in the masthead.

A newsletter readership survey conducted by a bank found that over half its respondents passed the newsletter along to an average number of three people. To ease and encourage further circulation, it immediately added a "route to" box on the first page of its newsletter.

Readers Seek Out Masthead

Often, readers search in the masthead for more information about your organization and how to contact you. Though you only have to write it once during the design stage, carefully word your masthead. Make it easy for readers to find the information they want. Use it as another place to promote your products and services.

The masthead gives the readers the information they need to know for correspondence along with identifying those who produced the publication. No matter how simple the newsletter, include a masthead listing:

➤ the name of the publication along with its subtitle

➤ its purpose

➤ the editor and organization

➤ your products or services

➤ your address

➤ your phone and facsimile number (if applicable)

➤ subscription costs (if any) and ordering information

➤ names of contributors

➤ copyright information or permission to reprint certain items

➤ frequency of publication

➤ disclaimers and lists of trademarks used

➤ volume and number

➤ deadline for copy if you accept contributions

Garden Getaway

This newsletter is published seasonally for River Road Nursery customers and neighbors. Readers are encouraged to submit questions, articles, and suggestions to the nursery. To be added to the mailing list, please complete the form below and mail or bring it to the nursery.

Name_____

Address_____

City_____ State____ Zip_____

River Road NURSERY   2625 River Road
Jefferson, LA 70121
837-7161

© 1990 River Road Nursery

To make your masthead more visually appealing, include the newsletter name as it appears in the nameplate. Box it off to make it easy to find. While there's no hard and fast rule on the placement of the masthead, try to keep it in the same place every issue.

Not all readers are familiar enough with formal publications to search out a masthead. For these readers, add your phone number and contact information in other places.

Sneaking in Your Phone Number & Contact Information

Discreetly print your organization's phone number whenever possible. Newsletters are notorious for their absence of phone numbers. Appropriate places for the phone number are in the masthead, under the return address on the mailing panel, and at the end of any article covering your products or services. Make sure your readers can contact you while the idea is fresh in their mind.

A dermatologist includes all of his office telephone numbers along with the location of his clinic on the back of every issue.

Depending on your type of business, you may also want to include your fax and telex numbers, hours, credit cards you accept, a list of your dealers, and a list of your products. Combine this information into your masthead, or create a special box that appears in every newsletter.

Often, promotional newsletter publishers summarize special events or product offerings in the form of an advertisement. Used sparingly, advertisements provide readers compartmentalized information without detracting from the news feel of your publications. Overuse, however, causes your newsletter to look like a brochure.

Sometimes you may not have enough room in your newsletter to provide prospects with all the information they need in order to make a purchase. Instead, give them the chance to request a brochure or arrange a personal visit. This is done using a reply card.

The Friends of City Park
cordially invite you
to attend
The Holiday Party
of

*Christmas
in the Oaks*

A City Park
Celebration

Thursday, December 6, 1990
7:00 p.m. - 10:00 p.m.
New Orleans
Botanical Garden
City Park
(Rain Site-NOMA)

A new Christmas tradition!
entertainment and exhibits,
lights, carousel and train rides.
Refreshments provided by
over 35 local restaurants
and caterers

Sponsored by
New Orleans Public Service, Inc.
and WWL-TV
$35.00 per person

cocktail attire
483-9415 or 483-7827

A non-profit organization announced a black tie event in the form of an advertisement. The ad made it simple for readers to find all the information about reservations and costs.

Boomerang Reply Card Designs

Design your reply cards to entice readers to mail them to you. Here's how:

> ➤ put the benefit of returning the card in large type
> ➤ list your telephone number for respondents who want to contact you immediately
> ➤ highlight the card with spot color or graphics
> ➤ make the card easy to remove from the newsletter and mail back

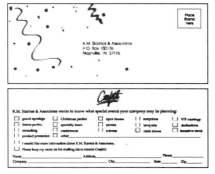

The reply card of *Confetti* uses the same design as in the rest of the newsletter.

If you use an inserted card, put your address on one side of the card. To return it to you, you can require readers to add a stamp. Or you can provide a business reply card that requires no postage. (Your post office can provide you with complete details on how to get a permit and produce your own business reply cards.)

The back of the card has space for the reader's name, organization, title, address and phone number. You can also add boxes to be checked off or space for the answers to a few simple questions. Leave plenty of room for respondents to write.

Some reply cards are stapled into the center of the newsletter. This assures that the card remains with the publication and is especially important for self-mailers. Many readers like the feeling of tearing out perforated cards. This may encourage interaction.

If the primary goal of your newsletter is to increase donations, include a reply card or a tear-out coupon in every issue. Supporters may want to donate mid-year or they may pass their newsletter along to an interested friend.

To improve the graphic appearance of your reply card and to add continuity to your newsletter's design, print it using the same colors or some of the same artwork as the body of your newsletter.

If you use a coupon, make it easy to remove by perforating around the edges. Make sure the address you want the respondent to reply to is listed on the coupon.

While this may seem to exhaust the possibilities for reader response, there's one last thing you can do.

'Til We Meet Again

Keep your promotion rolling. Encourage readers to look for the next newsletter by telling what it will offer. Include a "look for this in the next issue" list. Of course, some of your content is late breaking news that you can't predict. Just list a few upcoming features. By listing upcoming articles, you guide your climbers full circle back to recognition.

All of the design elements covered in this chapter help you attract and keep your prospect's attention. As you sit down to create each layout, choose the elements that best guide your readers through your publication. Turn the page to find out how.

12

The Self-Guided Promotional Tour

Ideally, you'd personally guide every reader through your newsletter. You'd point out what to read first and what not to miss. Practically speaking, though, you can't perch on the arm of every reader's chair.

Mail a road map instead. Chart your reader's course using the layout.

The layout is the arrangement of type and graphics on a page. It's different from design. In the design stages you choose the number of columns, typestyles for headlines and body copy, a nameplate and other design elements. These elements are the road signs of the layout. Arrange them on the page to create a self-guided tour up the mountain.

Most newsletter experts agree that if you fill a newsletter with information people desperately need, it doesn't matter how you present it. People will read the entire publication. However, promotional newsletters include both valuable information and promotional material.

Your primary concern when doing the layout of your newsletter is how to draw readers to your promotional features. Where do you place each article? What size should artwork be? How do you crop photos for the best effect? How do you fit in all of your articles?

If the layout artist isn't the newsletter editor, the editor must provide layout instructions. It's important to understand how readers interact with your printed page. Use this knowledge to guide your readers through every attraction at each promotional level.

How Readers Approach Your Mountain

Readers' eye movements help you chart your promotional tour. Readers approach an outer page differently than an inside spread. Within a single page, readers look at photos or illustrations first unless they are small. In the absence of photographs, readers' eyes are attracted by the largest and most dominant element on the page. Then they move to the second most dominant, then to the third, and so on. On a page of all text, readers' eyes usually move from the upper left to the lower right corner of the page in a "Z" pattern.

Only your first and last pages are seen by themselves. Other pages are usually seen as two-page spreads.

Most research on reader's eye movements has been conducted using magazines. In magazines, on a two-page spread, the reader's eye goes first to the right-hand page. Once readers glance over the right hand page, their eyes go to the left hand page. Both pages are read following the "Z" pattern.

This has not been studied in newsletters. The "Z" pattern also assumes that the elements on both pages are of equal interest. A key word in a headline or an interesting photograph can draw the readers' eyes to the left or to the bottom of the page.

Your job as the editor is to encourage readers to at least skim all elements of the newsletter. Begin articles on the tops of pages. Place your most important articles on the front page. Place photographs, graphics or needed industry information to draw readers first to the top left side of a spread. Realize,

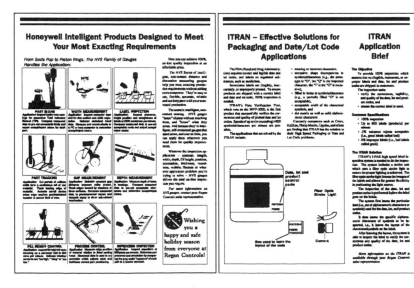

Most newsletters include lots of small bits of information. Take the most eye-catching bit and place it to the left of the spread. Your reader's eyes will naturally want to follow the "Z" pattern.

Place items on each page so that the layout follows this pattern.

though, that the top right hand of a spread is a powerful position. Place promotional items, such as new product or service announcements, here.

Another approach is to lure readers by using the front page for hard to find or useful information. Once you've captivated the readers, they'll turn to the inside pages filled with your promotional information.

Refugees Seek Political Freedom

If you have the same article running across two pages, you can create eye-catching graphics by placing the article across a spread. Use graphics and the headline to tie the pages together. Place a photograph near the beginning of the article to draw readers' eyes to the starting place.

Armed with better knowledge of eye movement, investigate how you can use the layout to guide your readers through each of the RISE levels—recognition, image, specifics and enactment.

You've already designed the standard sections of your newsletter for maximum appeal. The position of many of these features such as the nameplate and mailing panel will be the same from issue to issue. In the layout stages, use the areas *around* the standard features, the "active areas," to create appeal.

Creating "First Glance" Appeal

First, focus on the mailing panel and the front page. Your active areas on the mailing panel are the teasers or contents box. Highlight the items of greatest interest to your readers here. To attract attention, use:

> graphics
> spot color
> large type

A teaser placed in a colored box encourages recipients to become readers.

★✴➤▲●✴▼▼✴□ ★✴➤▲

5721 Magazine Street
New Orleans, LA 70115
(504) 283-6305

New
Products for
Desktop Publishing
see page 2

Next, look at your front page. Treat it like the cover of a magazine. Make it scream to be picked off the rack. Many newsletter editors face the challenge of working around standard features to create a new, exciting layout each time. While standard artwork or screened boxes add to recognition, the layout must cry out to readers, "This is a new issue!"

For example, the screened box in the newsletter to the left contains a standard news summary. With this type of design, the headline at the upper left and the graphic in the same column are the most important elements for attracting reader attention. Use your best headlines and artwork here to catch readers' eyes. Keep in mind that many readers expect the most important or newsworthy article to appear on the front page.

Layouts That Promote to Skimmers

Just as you need to attract attention from issue to issue, you must also create a "quick glance" version of your newsletter for skimmers. As mentioned in the beginning of the book, the appeal of newsletters is their conciseness.

The first step in creating a layout is to assume that no one will ever read a word of your body copy. Concentrate on pulling readers in and make your key points through interesting photographs and photo captions, headlines, pull quotes, subheads and decks. These elements can also be used to guide the reader from article to article throughout your newsletter.

First, you need to know your specific goals for each issue. These are the items, such as a new product or an upcoming event, that you want everyone who opens your newsletter to see. Don't bury these items deep within an article. Put them in a "skimmable" spot. These are essentially bypasses for "non-reading" readers.

Bypasses allow you to promote to the skimmers, and can bring your readers from image right into enactment. Shortcuts not only help the skimmers, but also help make your newsletter layout more pleasant for readers.

Let's look at some bypasses.

Cropping Photographs to Increase Interest

Since most readers look at photographs first, use photographs and captions to convey your most important promotional point. Cropping and other effects can increase their appeal. Your decisions in cropping depend upon what or who you are focusing on.

Cropping is important when photographing customers. A manufacturer wanted to show pictures of its customers who had won televisions in a contest. In several of the photos, only a part of the television was shown. It was all that was needed to communicate the idea. When space is at a premium, it's most important to make the image of the customer as large as possible.

Starr Brand Leads the Way in Boat Cover Manufacturing

Furney Irwin
Turner Marine

Troy & J.D. Whitaker
Sportsman's World

Starr Brand Inc. has manufactured boat covers and other marine products for almost twenty years. Although Starr manufactures Bimimis (free standing convertible boat tops) and boat tie downs used to strap boats to trailers, their primary product is boat covers. "We offer the largest selection of boat covers in the country," says Starr Brand executive vice president Gary Carver.

Their selection includes three basic types of covers: the universal, custom, and travel cover. The universal cover is a generic cover designed to fit all types of a specific class such as the 17 foot V-hull boat. Starr makes custom boat covers to fit boats made by particular manufacturers. The latest addition to the Starr cover line is the "Star Traveler" which is a towing cover for use while pulling a boat.

Marine distributors such as Mid South Marine comprise over 90% of their customer base, according to Carver. "Mid South Marine has been a valued customer almost as long as we've been in business," he explains. "Though they're not quite our biggest customer, they're our best. Mid South is very professional and thorough about their work and we appreciate that."

Donnie Dale receiving his Cancun tickets from Jeff Finley

Steve Slack
Lake Flite Marine

Randy Hooper
Boatland

Johnny Simerely
Johnny's Outboard

And The Winners Are...

Mid South Marine recently held a Starr Brand Boat Cover contest. Dealers submitted display pictures to *Boat and Motor Dealer* editor George Van Zeveren who judged the entries. Winners received a color T.V.

Also, Mid South representative Donnie Dale won a trip to Cancun, Mexico.

When cropping, first decide on your subject. Then, pull the reader into the subject by cropping the photograph. In the following photograph, if it's the man that's important, zoom in on the man. If it's the display, crop out the other people and center on the man's interest in the display. Note the angle of the man's body. It shows his interest and helps the photograph promote the display.

Full frame of photograph.

Man only.

Man and display.

Some photographs don't need cropping at all. The subject of this one was keeping track of the vast inventory at a video store. The person in the photograph makes the inventory size look very large.

Another effect that can add interest to a photograph is silhouetting. A silhouette is a cut out of only a part of the photograph. Many photographs lead readers' eyes in a specific direction. Use the motion of the photograph to pull readers' eyes into headlines or copy.

Silhouetting is also a useful effect for showing people. After all, most people aren't square or rectangular. By removing the background, the person looks more lifelike. Use this effect to show people from within your company. They'll look approachable and personable. Be aware, however, that silhouetting may cost you more money.

When using a caption, place it under or to the side of the photograph. Set it in large enough type to be easily read by skimmers.

Cars for Under $2,000 With Insect-Like Designs

The car of the future will weigh and cost no more than a $2,000 motorcycle, carry two to four people along with plenty of pigs and potatoes, and run on human, electric or motorcycle-engine power, says Italian-born German designer Luigi Colani during his Automotour '89 tour currently in the U.S.

This is because the automotive future lies in Asia, Africa and Indonesia, where 75 percent of the population lives. There, people are impowered by Western standards but car

sales will be one day counted in billions. "Automakers try to make things more complicated and expensive. We have to do it the other way around," he explains.

Colani even has designs for heavy trucks. To haul his Automotive concept cars, he has rebuilt a Mercedes-Benz tractor-trailer using 25

Continued on page 2

New Rates Go Into Effect February 6

A new UPS rate chart and UPS zone chart take effect on February 6.

Rates affected are UPS domestic ground service which will increase overall by 4.9 percent, ground service to Canada which increases 5.0 percent overall, and Next Day Air service which will go up 5.0 percent overall. UPS 2nd Day Air rates are unchanged. Also unchanged are rates for air service to Canada and International Air service. And the UPS Next Day Air Letter stays at the same low price, $8.50. UPS ground zone changes reflect U.S. Postal Service ZIP Code changes in

Florida and California. Included in the overall rate increases are the following changes in charges for additional services:
■ Weekly service charge increases from $3.75 to $4.00 per week
■ C.O.D. service — formerly $2.20, now $2.75
■ Acknowledgment of Delivery — was 35 cents, now 40 cents
■ Call Tag service increases from $1.15 to $1.25 (submitted in electronic transmission format — formerly 85 cents, now 90 cents)
■ Address corrections increase from $2.20 to $2.50

Prior to this increase, UPS

Next Day Air rates within the 48 states had not changed since the service began in 1982. 2nd Day Air rates have stayed the same since 1983. And UPS air service rates continue to be substantially lower than published rates of competing carriers.

If you have any questions about the changes in rates and zones, your UPS Customer Service representative will be glad to help.

No Change to Any of These Rates:
■ UPS Next Day Air Letter
■ UPS 2nd Day Air
■ Air service to Canada
■ International Air service

Effective Placement of Headlines & Subheads

By the time you get to the layout stage, you have already chosen attractive typestyles and written alluring captions, headlines, decks, pull quotes and subheads. Your job throughout the layout is to make sure the elements receive the best placement on the page.

You must also see that the typestyles and sizes stay consistent throughout the layout and aren't reduced or enlarged to fill up space. Use a consistent typeface, type size or alignment for all typographic elements. Be consistent in your headline positioning. Headlines reduced to fit available space instead of being edited might be mistaken for subheads. Short subheads enlarged to fill up space can be confused with headlines.

The layout of headlines is important. Headlines are one of the first elements noticed, so pay attention to the way multiple line headlines break in your layout. Bad breaks cause the meaning to change and robs the headline of promotional emphasis. Keep adjectives on the same line with the accompanying noun. Try not to end a line with a preposition.

Instead of breaking the headline like this:

**Up to Your Sleigh Bells in Christmas
Bills**

begin the second line with the preposition:

**Up to Your Sleigh Bells
in Christmas Bills**

You can use the breaks to emphasize certain words.

Every   makes a stronger statement than: **Every Vote Counts**
Vote
Counts

The headlines for your most important articles should span at least two columns. Use the largest type size you've chosen for major headlines. The size of the headline, along with the position of the article on a page, communicates the importance of the article.

Pull quotes on a page of all text add visual interest and gives you another chance to capture readers. Place the pull quote on the part of the page the eyes go to first, approximately at optical center (in the middle column, just above mathematical center).

If you have an interview written in question and answer format, the questions can work as subheads. Set questions in bold so readers can skim the questions and read the answers that interest them.

Don't separate headlines or subheads from the body of the article with lines or rules. Rules separate. The separation of subheads from the copy will make one article look like several different ones.

Highlight Items With Boxes & Graphics

If you have a promotional item that doesn't have an accompanying graphic or that isn't long enough for a full article, set it in a box.

A small article or advertisement, separated from the newsletter text by a box, is one way to promote to skimmers. To avoid offending readers, ads are usually placed on the back page.

In general, any item separated by a box draws attention. Some boxes draw more attention than others. Two point horizontal rules combined with one point vertical rules creates a contemporary box. Avoid vertical rules heavier than two point or scotch rules which look old-fashioned.

An option to using boxes is to separate the main items you want readers to see by white space. This forces a simple and uncluttered page. If only three elements are contained on a page, readers look at all three. The more elements you have, the less each is noticed.

If you have long articles in your newsletter, pull quotes, graphics and subheads are essential to guide those who read the text. They also guide the skimmers. Give skimmers something to look at on every page rather than page after page of text.

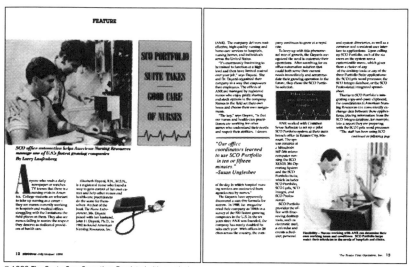

All elements on the page, including photographs, should work in harmony to tell skimmers the same story.

To Be Continued?

To attract skimmers' attention, some publications try to start as many articles as possible on the front page and continue them on the inside.

For promotional newsletters, however, take great care not to continue articles. Readers quickly tire from flipping through pages. They may stop reading your publication altogether. Having a set amount of space for each article encourages you to condense articles for maximum punch in minimum space.

If you have to continue an article, place the remainder on a facing page and use a jumpline. Jumplines tell where an article is continued or from where it came.

A Good Tour Guide for Readers

Make reading fun for your climbers. These people are working hard to grasp your message. All of the techniques used to create first glance appeal and communicate to skimmers also help guide "reading" readers.

The primary rule of layout is never allow your reader to get lost. An effective layout keeps elements organized and arranged in a logical order while having a strong focal point such as a promotional photo or headline.

Simple layouts are the best. They keep the pages uncluttered and straightforward. With limited elements on each page, you hold your reader's attention.

Layout involves the visual merging of words with graphics. While you use your graphics to promote your ideas, also use them to promote your words. The use of graphics on a page can direct eye flow through columns of text while making reading more fun and informative. This is done through:

➤ wrapping text around photographs and graphics

➤ using graphics to keep readers' eyes in the most important areas of the page

➤ signaling the beginning of articles with initial caps or graphics

➤ guiding readers with arrows, photographs, kickers and more

Graphics can be included in an article layout by boxing them off, wrapping text around them.

This newsletter involves the photographs with the articles by wrapping text around them.

If your graphic interferes with reading the copy, consider using it as part of the headline instead.

Show readers your enthusiasm for the article. Begin with the contents box. Repeat a graphic that runs throughout the story. Then, use a graphic along with subheads or charts to visually tie the article together. The longer the article, the more important it is to sustain interest using graphic tools.

Other tools are used to guide readers through the layout. To signal the beginning of new articles, you can start each article with a large or stylized letter, called an initial cap. Initial caps are usually used as the first letter of the first line of text. However, don't use initial caps if you have lots of short items on a page. The page quickly becomes spotty.

A stylized letter is used by a nursery's newsletter in the first letter of each headline. The floral style of the script is consistent with the ambiance of the newsletter.

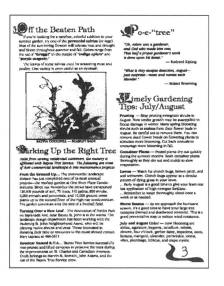

Discrimination

Action Based on 'Perception' of Individual as Handicapped is Discriminatory

by Matthew C. Lonergan

A Federal District Court in California recently ruled that an individual who tested AIDS seropositive and was discharged from a hospital's alcohol and drug rehabilitation program was protected as handicapped under the 1973 Rehabilitation Act.

The hospital excluded all seropositive individuals from the inpatient treatment program because of the infection risk associated with communicable diseases, especially the risk of AIDS transmission through sexual contact or intravenous drug use.

In order to qualify as handicapped, an individual must show: (1) he is an individual with a handicap; (2) he is "otherwise qualified" for the program of benefits from which he was excluded; (3) he was excluded solely because of his handicap; and (4) the program is subject to the Rehabilitation Act. In this instance, because the hospital received Medicare funds, it was subject to

section 504 of the Act. Moreover, the Act protects from discrimination individuals who are actually handicapped, as well as those who are "perceived" by others to be handicapped. Regardless of whether the seropositive individual...

INSIDE

Use your contents box along with kickers to guide readers. A law office gets readers' attention by listing topics in its "inside" box. To make it easy for readers to find the story inside, the editor uses the same wording as a kicker for the article.

Volume 2 No. 3

SmartWare® INK

THE INNOVATIVE SOFTWARE NEWSLETTER

CONTENTS

INNOVATIVE SOFTWARE AND AT&T RELEASE SMARTWARE FOR 3B SERIES

Innovative Software and AT&T have announced the release of SmartWare for the AT&T 3B line of computers, including the 3B2/400, 510, 400, 600, 595, and the 3B15.

Smart for the 3B series is a UNIX product marketed by AT&T Computer Systems Division. It is available only from AT&T.

The Smart Software System for AT&T's 3B series provides users the power of the 32-bit UNIX family combined with the benefits afforded by a complete set of business productivity applications.

Smart takes full advantage of the UNIX multiuser environment including file and record locking in The Smart Data Base Manager, and file locking in The Smart Spreadsheet with Business Graphics and The Smart Word Processor.

The 3B family includes machines of the supermicro and supermini class. AT&T provides several options for networking the 3B series. Options include wide area (local) area networking capability and mainframe connectivity. The AT&T StarLan

is the premier solution for DOS/UNIX connectivity, permitting DOS and UNIX terminals to exchange data on the same local area network.

Two important advantages of The Smart Software System are a common user interface and the ability to exchange data between DOS and UNIX environments. This permits applications originally created in the DOS environment to be easily moved into the more powerful UNIX environment, without the need for conversion utilities or retraining.

INNOVATIVE SOFTWARE SIGNS AGREEMENT WITH MERRILL LYNCH

Innovative Software, Inc. has announced a formal agreement with Merrill Lynch and Co. Under terms of the agreement, Innovative will provide Merrill Lynch with a version of The Smart Software System designed for use on a series of intelligent broker workstations.

The workstations will provide brokers with the ability to analyze client portfolios and perform what-if analysis using stock market data.

The Smart Software System is an integral part of the intelligent broker workstation, providing the power and flexibility to integrate quote retrieval and portfolio analysis. ∎

1

In several ways, the design of this page is inviting. The "thumb print" area to the right encourages you to hold the newsletter. The large initial cap "I" says, "Start here." If the reader isn't interested in the first article, another begins just one column away. And, the remainder of the contents are listed close by.

Squeezing or Expanding to Fit

What if your copy is too long to include eye-leading graphics? What if you have too little copy and the layout looks awkward? The following are some tips to help you finish your layout without sacrificing your newsletter's promotional punch.

If you don't have enough space for everything to fit:

➤ tightly edit your copy

➤ look for widows and orphans (short words appearing as the final line of a paragraph or the first line of a column, respectively)

➤ reword sentences

➤ remove subheads

➤ break the article into two parts; continue the article next time

➤ remove graphics and photographs

➤ if you have two related pictures for an article and one of the photos has some dead space in it, superimpose one picture onto another

➤ make graphics or photographs smaller

➤ crop photos judiciously

➤ shorten headlines

➤ justify text and hyphenate

If you have too much blank space left over:

➤ add a pull quote

➤ enlarge photographs or graphics

➤ leave one column empty and place pull quote or graphic here

➤ add subheads

➤ box in an article and decrease the column width of text

➤ add divider lines

➤ run text ragged right

➤ scallop the bottom of the layout in a three-column format

➤ effectively incorporate white space into the page design

Desktop publishing systems ease many layout traumas. They let you see automatically how the changes you make affect the layout.

Through effective layout of each page, you entertain your climbers as they move through the most strenuous part of the climb. You guide and encourage them to interact with your newsletter in hopes they discover the information they need to stay on the tour for the last part of the climb.

The Last Stop on the Tour

Although you may have designed a standard reply card for each issue in the design stages, as you do the layout of each issue you may want readers to respond to a specific offer or promotion. If so, create a special response request. You can:

➤ place a coupon near a special article

➤ loosely insert a reply card

➤ staple a card in the center of the newsletter

Coupons placed near articles encourage readers to respond immediately after they've read the copy. By taking advantage of your readers' momentum, you may increase your response.

In a direct marketing newsletter, a perforated reply coupon was underneath an article on a special offer for a calculator. The photograph used in the text was also placed on the coupon. The newsletter was printed on heavy paper so the coupon could be cut out and mailed without an envelope.

Like any good guide, you're going to learn from your climbers. Use this knowledge to improve your tour. Take note of the comments and responses you receive from your readers. Try to determine what it is that reached your audience. The variables are great. It could be the topic of an article, the way a headline was worded, an interesting photo , the way you designed your reply card, or a mixture of all of these.

Be an innovative guide. Experiment with your own ideas. If you have a hunch about what might attract readers, give it a try. Let experience with your prospects change and evolve your newsletter. Readers will sense your increased involvement in their needs. That alone is a powerful promotional message.

There are other ways to evolve your newsletter beyond a printed medium. The next chapter gives you a few ideas.

13

Newsletters of the Future

Many futuristic projections never become reality. If they did, the bulk of this book would explain how to send your newsletter over an electronic bulletin board rather than printing and mailing it. And you'd probably be reading this from your computer monitor instead of holding it in your hands.

But some facts are hard to ignore. Statistics from the U.S. Labor Department show that about half the work force is under 35 years of age. Countless studies confirm that these people, born after the family television set became a household fixture, are more comfortable receiving information electronically or in face-to-face discussions than in print.

To capture the attention of this growing segment of the population, you may consider taking the news printed in your newsletter and recording it onto other formats.

Electronic Newsletters

Often, it's difficult to project how new technology will be used. My father remembers when television first became available. His mother wasn't interested in buying one. She said she preferred listening to the radio over watching someone read the script.

The use of most current technology is easier to see than it was for my grandmother to imagine the benefits of television.

News on Hold. Instead of silence or music, you can record a cassette tape of tips and information from your current newsletter for callers to listen to while on hold. This reinforces the messages printed in your newsletter.

Newsletters on Cassette. The newsletter recording made for your on-hold listeners can also be copied and distributed for prospects to listen to while traveling in their car. *All Things Considered*, a radio program aired on most public broadcasting stations, is essentially a radio newsletter.

One company, Microcomputer Newstapes of Westminster, MA, is using cassette tapes to distribute its monthly magazine spotlighting trends, technologies and people in the computer industry. The tapes consist of 90 minutes of interviews and commentaries, and are sold on a subscription basis.

Radio Spots. If your newsletter has mass appeal, record an interview or one of the articles from your publication and distribute it to radio stations as a public service announcement. The station may air it free or you can buy air time. The spot should run between 30 seconds and two minutes.

Electronic Bulletin Boards. If you already have an electronic bulletin board set up for technical support, you can include your newsletter along with other information. One advantage of having your newsletter on a bulletin board is that users can leave a message if they have a question about what they've just read. This way, your newsletter is a true form of two-way communication.

If you don't have your own bulletin board, you may be able to add it to someone else's. For example, Mead Data Central, in Dayton, OH, operates NEXIS, a on-line information retrieval system for newsletters.

Desktop Media and Video Tapes. The concept of desktop publishing has been expanded into a concept called desktop media. Desktop media gives publishers the power to not only produce published documents but also color slides and animation. For example, the technology already exists to produce a video solely by computer and recorded on standard video tape. Conceivably, your newsletter could be recorded and distributed to your customers and prospects.

Videos can also be recorded using video cameras. Some organizations, such as Amnesty International, distribute almost as many video tapes as they do printed pieces. Because the organization focuses on human rights, it finds showing tapes of people more descriptive than printed words.

Newsletters Sent via Facsimile. Services already exist to send bulk facsimile transmissions. With postage rates going up and telephone line charges staying competitive, it may be a cost-effective method of distribution.

Using Newsletter Information in Other Printed Pieces

In addition to electronic formats, many newsletters can be expanded into other printed forms. These may come in handy once your newsletter has established itself.

Magazines. If your newsletter expands dramatically, you may want to convert it to a magazine. This is not common, however, since most newsletters remain newsletters because they are put to uses that are impossible or impractical for larger publications. Further, most newsletters cost less to produce than magazines.

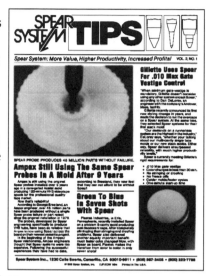

If budget is no concern, the advantage of publishing a magazine is image. What can do more to build the image of an organization than a four color magazine? For example, one manufacturer publishes a quarterly publication. It is published in German, French and Japanese. The print run for the U.S. edition is 40,000 and the other language editions exceed 10,000 each. The magazine format also allows the sponsor to include more than 40 pages of advertisements per issue.

Many ads are using longer informational copy, complete with subheads. It may be feasible to take a new product article and use the copy in an advertisement.

In addition, pharmaceutical companies often sponsor scientific journals where basic research can be published.

Annual Reports. For publicly-held companies, much of the information published in the newsletter during the year can be used for the annual report. This is a timely concept since many annual reports are being designed with a news format versus the traditional look of an annual report.

One annual report looked so much like a newspaper, it got its sponsor in trouble. The publishers of *USA TODAY* insisted that the erring corporation publicly apologize for copying their design.

Press Releases. Many newsletter articles, especially those on new products, can be reformatted slightly and used as press releases.

Apply Techniques to All Promotional News

The potential versatility of newsletter formats gives you many options when choosing how to present your product news to customers and prospects. Perhaps it's only suiting that the newsletter, one of the first communication forms to take advantage of the printing press, should also be the one to adapt to new technology such as desktop publishing and desktop media.

Regardless of the format you choose for your newsletter, be it printed, transmitted, or recorded, the basic principles for its creation are the same. Keep in sight your own goals and march them alongside the needs of your prospects.

Use this concept in conjunction with the four steps of RISE. Create a message that begins with **Recognition**. Give the basic information needed to know you. Move on by conveying your **Image**, including your products, services and ideas. Lead prospects a step further with **Specifics** by explaining complex products and services. Then, inspire them to take the final step of **Enactment**.

Do this and the publication you create will be a successful, promotional newsletter.

Atop the Mountain: a Few Final Words

It's my biggest hope that this book has churned the creative juices within you. You have all the tools you need to create the ideal publication for your organization.

Just think "promotion." As I searched for examples for each part of this book, I was drawn to the same publications again and again. The ones with effective names had great nameplate designs. The newsletters with communicative graphics had great headlines and captions.

That's because once you start thinking promotion, it will show in every aspect of your promotional newsletter.

A APPENDIX

7 Steps for Choosing the Right Vendors

A keen ability to hire good employees makes for a good business. The same is true for hiring newsletter subcontractors. Professionals should deliver the job as specified, on the day it's due, and at the price originally quoted. It's simply a matter of finding talented subcontractors who run good businesses.

To find good vendors, follow these steps.

1. **Review Samples of Previous Work Every Time You Hire a New Vendor.** Ask for samples you can keep. Compare your newsletter to other samples periodically. When choosing writers and designers, make sure their style fits your organization's image. When considering a printer, look for smudge-free printing, high-resolution photographs, and even folding.

    As you are looking at the vendor's work and asking questions, make sure your subcontractor is asking *you* questions. People who ask questions back are listening to what you want.

2. **Look for Hardware and Software Compatibility.** If you're doing any part of your newsletter production yourself, you'll want to find vendors who have computer systems compatible with yours.

    For example, if you're writing the articles yourself and sending them to a desktop publishing service or typesetter for layout, choose one that can get the information off your disk instead of having to rekey the information. If you take articles from a writer and lay them out on your in-house system, get the writer to use a disk size and format that you can use with your computer.

Electronic storage is also important for mailing labels and printing. If a mailing service has the capabilities, they can take your database on disk and print out the labels for you. Many printers have the equipment to take your complete newsletter on disk, print it out on a laser printer or typesetting equipment, and send it directly to be printed. As many printers also have mailing services, the same disk with your newsletter layout may also contain your mailing list.

3. **Check References.** Note the pieces you like. Ask for the name and phone number of the person who commissioned the work. Call that person to see if there were any problems and if he or she would use the vendor's services again. For creative services, it's important to find out how much direction was given by the client. Someone else may have edited the work extensively to get it into the form that's catching your eye.

   Interviewing others who have used a specific service will give you some guidelines in case you decide to work with the vendor despite potential problems. For instance, if you hear that a project went over budget, you may take extra precautions to secure a firm quote.

4. **Request Price Quotes and Turnaround Times.** Prices vary tremendously from vendor to vendor. Some mailing services, for example, have minimum orders. If you're mailing a small job, find one that doesn't have a minimum. Some printers have certain size orders or formats they specialize in. If you fit within their speciality, they'll give you a competitive bid. If you don't, shop around. Also keep in mind that most services can't give you a firm price until they see the exact job.

5. **Involve Subcontractors in Planning.** Be sure to tell the prospective vendor about any idiosyncrasies or taboos—policies, design standards—which will automatically cause you to reject work. If you're set on having something done a specific way, tell your vendor. Since most subcontractors bill hourly, you can save money by giving specific instructions.

6. **Establish Turnaround Time and the Final Deadline.** This will allow you to make a realistic schedule. Allow extra time to compensate for miscommunications, and allow extra money to cover changes you may need to make in the final work—but only for changes from what was decided at the project's onset. In such cases, the vendor deserves to be paid extra for revisions and alterations, at a previously agreed rate. If you catch yourself making frequent revisions in assignments, rethink your planning process and how you are giving instructions to all involved.

Set interim deadlines so you can make sure the project is on the right track. For all newsletter services, revisions are easier and less expensive to make at earlier stages. In the worst case, you can make alternate arrangements if you feel a vendor isn't working out. At each interim check, make sure you reconfirm the final deadline.

7. **Set and Agree Upon the Total Fee for the Job.** Do this immediately upon assigning the work. If the fee is not a flat amount, agree upon the formula you will use in determining the total cost for the project. Flat fees are preferable because they encourage the subcontractor to work as efficiently as possible, potentially saving *your* time and money in the process. Discuss who pays for materials and other services such as typesetting, film, processing and retouching. Also discuss payment terms.

Agree on the exact form in which the work will be delivered. Put your agreements in writing and have your vendor sign the contract. People have a tendency to pay more attention to the things they have to sign.

For creative services, agree on who owns the copyrights. In the absence of an agreement stating otherwise, the freelancer owns all copyrights to the work produced and you are paying for one-time usage. You can negotiate complete rights, usage under specific conditions, or the ability to make derivative works. If you decide on one time use, agree upon the fees you'll pay for additional uses.

When negotiating fees with subcontractors, You may avoid set-up fees or negotiate a lower fee per issue by agreeing to sign a year contract. The contract will commit you to a certain number of newsletters per year. For the vendor, it offsets the extra time involved in working on a new project by assuring year-long business. As with printers, don't sign a yearly contract until you're satisfied with the first issue.

B APPENDIX

Books & Other Resources

Books on Newsletters

Editing Your Newsletter
by Mark Beach
Coast to Coast Books
Portland, OR
General reference for newsletter editors.

Newsletter Editor's Desk Book
Marvin Arth & Helen Ashmore
Parkway Press
Shawnee Mission, KS
Journalistic guide for newsletter editors.

Newsletters From the Desktop
Roger C. Parker
Ventana Press
Chapel Hill, NC
Newsletter designing and layout with a computer.

Outstanding Newsletter Designs
Polly Pattison, Mary Pretzer & Mark Beach
Coast to Coast Books
Portland, OR
Shows 65 sample publications.

Publishing Newsletters
Howard Penn Hudson
Charles Scribner's Sons
New York, NY
If you want to turn your newsletter into a subscription publication.

Success in Newsletter Publishing
Frederick Goss
Newsletter Association
Arlington, VA
Covers for-profit, subscription newsletters.

Books on Writing

Associated Press Stylebook
Christopher French
Addison-Wesley Publishing Co.
Reading, MA.

Content Ideas That Work
Mark Beach
Coast to Coast Books
Portland, OR

Edit Yourself: A manual for everyone who works with words
Bruce Ross-Larson
W.W. Norton & Co.
New York, NY

The Elements of Style
William Strunk Jr. and E.B. White
MacMillan Publishing Co., Inc.
New York, NY

If You Want to Write
Brenda Ueland
Graywolf Press
St. Paul, MN

Make Every Word Count
Gary Provost
Writer's Digest Books
Cincinnati, OH

Public Relations Writing
Robert Rayfield, et al
Wm. C. Brown Publishers
Dubuque, IA

Books on Design

Designer's Guide to Creating Charts & Diagrams
Nigel Holmes
Watson-Guptill Publications
New York, NY

Editing by Design
Jan V. White
R.R. Bowker Company
New York, NY

Page Design Templates

Page Designs Quick
(120 templates for 3- and 4-column newsletters)

Page Designs 5
(225 templates for 5-column tabloid newspapers)
Mac & PC versions for PageMaker
PAR Publishing Co.
6355 Topanga Canyon Blvd., #307
Woodland Hills, CA 91367
(818) 340-8165

Style Sheets for Newsletters: A guide to advanced design on Xerox Ventura Publisher
by Martha Lubow & Polly Pattison
Pattison Workshops
5092 Kingscross Rd.
Westminster, CA 92683
(714) 894-8143

Cartoons

Cartoons by Johns
Box 1300
Pebble Beach, CA 93953
(408) 649-0303

Creative Media Services
Box 5955
Berkley, CA 94705
(415) 843-3408

Farcus Cartoons, Inc.
Box 3006, Station C
Ottawa, Canada K1Y 4J3
(613) 235-5944

Grantland Enterprises
305 N. Mountain Ave.
Upper Montclair, NJ 07043

Stock Photography Sources

Stock Photo Deskbook
The Photographic Arts Center
163 Amsterdam Ave., #201
New York, NY 10023
(212) 838-8640

Stock Photography Handbook
ASMP
419 Park Ave. So.
New York, NY 10016
(212) 889-9144

Stock Workbook
Scott & Daughters Publishing
940 N. Highland Ave.
Los Angeles, CA 90038
(800) 547-2688
(213) 856-0008

Library of Congress
Prints and Photos Division
Washington, DC 20540
(202) 707-6394

Museum of Modern Art
Film Stills Archive
11 W. 53rd St.
New York, NY 10019
(212) 708-9480

Bettman Archive (UPI photos & others)
902 Broadway, 5th Floor
New York, NY 10010
(212) 777-6200

Scanned Photographs

COMSTOCK Desktop Photography
30 Irving Pl.
New York, NY 10003
(212) 353-8686

DiscImagery
18 E. 16th Street
New York, NY 10003
(212) 675-8500

On-Line News Services

BRS Information Technologies
1200 Route 7
Latham, NY 12110
(518) 783-1161
More than 80 databases in the areas of business and finance, education, reference, science and medicine, and the social sciences.

Dialog Information Services, Inc.
3460 Hillview Ave.
Palo Alto, CA 94304
(415) 858-3792
Offers more than 200 databases that reference more than 50 million articles in over 60,000 printed publications from around the world in a variety of broad categories. Also offer Knowledge Index, a scaled-down, less expensive version that operates only after prime time hours.

Dow Jones News/Retrieval Service
P.O. Box 300
Princeton, NJ 08543
(609) 520-4000
On-line service offering financial and general databases.

Legi-Slate
777 North Capitol St., N.E., Suite 900
Washington, DC 20002
(202) 898-2300
Electronic legislative bill-tracking service.

Mead Data Central
9393 Springboro Pike, Bldg. 2
P.O. Box 933
Dayton, OH 45401
(513) 865-6800
Legal information databases, 14 newspapers, 39 magazines, 12 wire services, 50 newsletters, the Encyclopedia Britannica, and more.

NewsNet
945 Haverford Rd.
Bryn Mawr, PA 19010
(215) 527-8030
More than 300 newsletters in 32 categories, also offers many news wires.

Seminars on Newsletters

DGEF (Dynamic Graphics Educational
Foundation)
6000 North Forest Park Dr.
Peoria, IL 61614
(800) 255-8800
(309) 688-8866

Editorial Experts, Inc.
66 Canal Center Plaza, Suite 200
Alexandria, VA 22314-1538
(703) 683-0683

Newsletter Clearinghouse
44 West Market St.
Rhinebeck, NY 12572
(914) 876-2081

The Newsletter Factory
1640 Powers Ferry Rd., Bldg. 8, #110
Marietta, GA 30067
(404) 955-2002

Padgett-Thompson
11221 Roe Ave.
Leawood, KS 66211
(800) 255-4141
(913) 451-2900

Pattison Workshops
5092 Kingscross Rd.
Westminster, CA 92683
(714) 894-8143

Promotional Perspectives
1955 Pauline Blvd., Suite 100-A
Ann Arbor, MI 48103
(313) 994-0007

Ragan Communications
407 S. Dearborn St.
Chicago, IL 60605
(800) 878-5333
(312) 922-8245

Associations

The Newsletter Association
1401 Wilson Blvd., Suite 403
Arlington, VA 22209
(703) 527-2333

National Assoc. of Desktop Publishers
P.O. Box 508, Kenmore Station
Boston, MA 02215-9998
(617) 437-6472

Intl. Assoc. of Business Communicators
One Hallidie Plaza, Suite 600
San Francisco, CA 94102
(415) 433-3400

Public Relations Society of America
33 Irving Place
New York, NY 10003-2376
(212) 995-2230

Magazines & Newsletters

Before & After
PageLab
331 J St., #150
Sacramento, CA 95814
(916) 443-4890

Communications Briefings
P.O. Box 587
Glassboro, NJ 08028
(800) 888-2084

Communications Concepts
Box 1608
Springfield, VA 22151

Desktop Communications
P.O. Box 941727
Atlanta, GA 30341
(800) 966-9052; (404) 493-4786

Editorial Eye
66 Canal Center Plaza, Suite 200
Alexandria, VA 22314-1538
(703) 683-0683

Editor's Forum
Box 1806
Kansas City, MO 64141
(913) 236-9235

Inhouse Graphics
4550 Montgomery Ave., #700
Bethesda, MD 20814

Newsletter Design
44 West Market Street
Rhinebeck, NY 12572
(914) 876-2081

**Newsletters News:
Ideas & inspiration for
promotional newsletters**
EF Communications
6614 Pernod Ave.
St. Louis, MO 63139-2149
(800) 264-6305

The Newsletter Newsletter
Communication Resources
P.O. Box 2625
North Canton, OH 44720
(216) 499-1950
For editors of church newsletters.

Newsletter on Newsletters
44 West Market Street
Rhinebeck, NY 12572
(914) 876-2081

The Page
Box 14493
Chicago, IL 60614

Publish
P.O. Box 55400
Boulder, CO 80322
(800) 274-5116; (303) 447-9330

Ragan Report
407 South Dearborn Street
Chicago, IL 60605
(312) 922-8245

Credits

The following newsletters were reprinted in this book with the permission of their publishers.

Production
Notes

The typeface used in this book is Garamond 11 point with 13.5 point leading. The headlines, subheads, captions, and sidebar text are in Franklin Gothic. Page folios and secondary subheads are in ITC Kabel.

The text of the book was entered into Microsoft Word 4.0. Most examples and all cartoons were scanned with an Epson ES-300C scanner. Scanned images were touched up using Desk Paint or Image Studio. All elements were placed into the page format using PageMaker and a Macintosh II. Pages were printed on a Linotronic L230.

The cover was designed by Joe Mariano using Design Studio. The film containing the color separations was printed on a L230 by Graphics Unlimited, New Orleans, LA.

Photographs of the book (before it actually was a book) were made by printing the cover design directly onto photographic film at Dennis Carney Photography, Nashville, TN.

Index

About
the Ducks

Rufus (with glasses) and the ducks shown in a rare moment of relaxation. This photograph was scanned using a Bulgo3000XYZ and retouched in the wee hours of the morning using soft feathers, explaining the poor focus.

Photo: Dennis Carney

About the Author

Elaine Floyd is president of EF Communications, formerly a newsletter writing and production service that developed over 50 different newsletters for all types of organizations.

Currently, EF Communications publishes books and a subscription newsletter for other promotional newsletter editors.

Upcoming projects include booklets for vertical markets—banking, legal, retail, medical, non-profit—showing newsletters along with discussing the special marketing needs for each type of organization.

Also, ready for launch, is a subscription newsletter on promotional newsletters, *Newsletter News: ideas & inspiration for promotional newsletters.* There's a coupon for a free issue in the back of this book.